Growing Up Gingerly

Growing Up Gingerly

Kathy White

Unending appreciation to
Bob and Cheryl
for providing a safe haven.

CONTENTS

DEDICATION   v

GROWING UP GINGERLY

1   The Kindness of Strangers   3

2   Janet's Laugh   6

3   My Father's Shop   12

4   The Shoeshine Box   16

5   Pumpkin Head and the Tramp   19

PRESSURE POINTS

6   There's a Wheel in My Nose   25

7   Miss Hyde   27

8   Keys to the Car   30

9   The Brown Paper Bag   34

CONTENTS

10 ┃ I Am Not You   38

FRESH AIR

11 ┃ Making Hay While the Sun Shines, Part 1   43

12 ┃ Making Hay While the Sun Shines, Part 2   48

13 ┃ The Pink Paint   52

14 ┃ Trashy Reading Material   57

15 ┃ Darn Those Socks   60

ENCHANTMENT AND DISENCHANTMENT

16 ┃ The Yellow Room   65

17 ┃ Barbie Bubbling Spa   68

18 ┃ Field Report   72

19 ┃ Prom Princess in a Convertible   77

FLYING HIGH

20 ┃ Anecdote and Antidote   83

21 | Ecstasy   90

22 | How to Lie with Statistics   94

23 | Love at a Price   98

24 | Meeting David Johnston   105

MOVING ON

25 | Making Drapes   111

26 | The Mystery Building: A New Perspective   115

27 | Trouble with a Water Flosser   119

28 | Hidden Treasure   123

29 | My Filter Queen   126

HEADY VERSES

ABOUT THE AUTHOR   139
ACKNOWLEDGEMENTS   141

GROWING UP GINGERLY

GROWING UP GINGERLY

The Kindness of Strangers

At five years of age, I was shy but self-assured and independent. I knew what I was and was not capable of, and I was always on the lookout for a better way to do things.

I watched my father carefully, and he amazed me with his innate ability to figure out a new solution to a challenge, like using a lever to lift something that was bigger than he was. It later occurred to me that this was natural for a man who was only five foot two at his tallest. Inheriting his genetics, and following his example, I constantly looked for opportunities to make my life easier.

One time this was a dresser. No one had to point out to me that the open drawers of a dresser made a handy set of stairs, especially if you were trying to reach something on the top shelf of the closet nearby.

The trick worked a few times, and then one night—*bam!*—the dresser toppled forward as I climbed up its drawers. Luckily, it didn't fall on top of me. Shaken but unhurt, I decided to report this to my father in the living room. He seemed not to have heard the big noise. More surprising, he didn't seem at all concerned about the incident. My father simply righted the dresser. Clearly I had learned my lesson.

Another time, I was coming home from school. It was spring, and I was wearing cloudy-grey overshoes that we called puddlers.

They were foot-shaped envelopes of translucent plastic that pulled across and over the top of the foot. They fastened shut with a black elastic loop around a metal stud.

In the 1960s, boots were called overshoes—they were actually worn over your shoes. Puddlers were lighter than the big winter boots we called galoshes, which had small flat buckles that pulled easily through a metal slot. But puddlers were harder to do up, owing to the elastic loop. It was tempting not to bother. You could get outside and moving faster by leaving them open.

I discovered during my first year of school that it took a considerable amount of time to walk out the kindergarten doors, turn left along the bike racks to the street, then take a right along the sidewalk toward my home. A shortcut across the corner of the schoolyard saved valuable time as well as the effort of going all the way round. In winter, this was hard because of the snow, but it was spring, and the snow had cleared. What I didn't account for as I headed across the shortcut towards the sidewalk was the mud. It was much deeper than it looked.

I blithely strode out into the muddy section, realizing a bit late that the effort of lifting my feet out of the mud outweighed the inconvenience of going around. But never mind. On I trod, focused on the path in front of me—*schluck, schluck, schluck*. It was hard going. I had made it just past half-way when I looked down and realized that I was wearing only one puddler.

I was tired from a long afternoon at school, and I could barely lift my feet up and out of the mud. I tried not to cry, but as I looked around, I had no idea what to do next. The spectre of my mother's reaction to a muddy shoe and lost puddler was lurking in the back of my mind, right behind the challenge of getting out of this mess.

My independence was such that I never asked for help. Luckily a kind boy, possibly a Grade Seven student, noticed my predicament.

He lifted me up and carried me the few yards to the safety of the bare, dry sidewalk. Then, miracle of miracles, realizing that my other puddler was still stuck in the middle of the muddy patch, he rescued that, too. Then he disappeared from my sight. I still have no idea who he was, where he came from, or where he went afterwards.

I made my way home and stood on the front step of our bungalow. I had removed both puddlers by this time and held them behind my back in one hand. Surely my mother would not see my muddy shoe if I hid the overshoes from sight. I chose to ring the doorbell, which might have been a signal to my mother that something wasn't quite right.

When my mother opened the door that day, she surprised me. I quietly pleaded, "Promise not to get mad?" Looking at my shoe, caked with dried mud, she didn't chide me. She didn't demand an explanation or ascribe blame. Without a word, she took my shoe and the puddlers. I was so certain that she would be angry and inconvenienced. I expected harsh words and a spanking for my carelessness. But she kindly helped me fix a problem of my own making—without recrimination or retribution.

I still remember that nameless boy who rescued me. He remains a true hero in my sentimental mind. But looking back at that day, I wonder if my mother wasn't the real unsung hero. That particular day, she didn't make a fuss. She seemed to understand that I had already been humbled and had learned my lesson. I needed kindness and assistance, not discipline.

Janet's Laugh

Robert Godby leaned toward me with his flaming red hair and freckles and yowled, "My parents wouldn't buy the class picture! Because of YOU!"

The picture was our Grade Two class photo, the standard 1960s black-and-white, five-by-seven. Everyone was dressed up that day. The short kids, including me, sat humbly in the front row, while the tall kids stood awkwardly on the wooden benches at the back.

The backdrop was always the same—the stage in the school gym. In the front, a small blackboard announced the teacher, school, and year, as well as the photographer, Murray Studios.

In the front row of this particular photo, though, was a crazed-looking child with bulging eyes, a face full of freckles, missing teeth, and frizzy, home-permed hair that could only be red. This, sad to say, was me. And beside me was the pretty smiling face of my friend, Janet Rothwell.

It was, in fact, Janet's fault that the photo was ruined, that I looked like a reason for Robert Godby's parents not to buy it. Janet had said to me, "If you laugh when they take the picture, it will look like a smile." I believed her. And it was true for her, but for me, well, not so much.

It was bad enough in those days to be cursed with red hair and freckles. My impulsive and maniacal behaviour had compounded the situation. Robert Godby, too, suffered from being both ginger and impulsive. A few weeks earlier, he had turned around in line and given me a big, wet kiss. I was shocked when Mrs. Nute slammed him against the wall and yelled at him. This was an extreme reaction, even for Mrs. Nute.

* * *

That year, Janet and I called ourselves "tabernacle buddies," bonded by the outrageous good fortune of being allowed to walk, by ourselves, downtown to the public library.

On alternate Tuesdays, as soon as school was over, we would wade through the throngs of children in the schoolyard, cross the lime-lined football field, and continue into a wooded area surrounding a creek that wound its way past my house in the suburbs toward downtown. Beyond the school boundaries, the creek descended for the length of a shady, five-minute walk, bubbling over the limestone slabs as we passed between the backyards of the houses to emerge onto Front Avenue.

From there we turned left onto the wide and busy Stewart Boulevard, which led downtown. A final block past the Shell station brought us to the overpass across the railroad tracks between Toronto and Montreal, on the other side of which Stewart Boulevard mysteriously became William Street.

The overpass seemed immense to us and was quite a climb. The train tracks were at street level, so the road had to rise high over them before descending back to street level on the other side. From the top of the overpass, we could see the tracks stretching into the distance each way. We didn't pay much attention to the freight trains when they passed under us—we knew them well enough from long waits in our hot cars at level crossings. Sometimes we would see freight or passenger cars, as well as handcars, parked on the sidings.

From the overpass, we could see pretty much from one end of the town to the other. Mysterious objects of all sorts were littered along the tracks and in the yards behind the houses and other buildings that lined the railway property. The yards were more interesting than our own backyards with their mowed lawns and swing sets. When there was no train passing through, we could hear strange banging sounds and gruff voices that seemed to come from nowhere. And there were no other children's voices to be heard, just ours.

In the summer, the steep, grassy slopes of the overpass would yield soft-drink bottles, which we would cart to the Corner Lunch on the next block. In the days of the five-cent allowance, this was a windfall: we cashed in the small pop bottles for two cents and the large ones for five. This ready money was immediately spent on candy. The Corner Lunch had two large glass cases of colourful sugary treats. Black balls were my favourite. They were three for a penny and changed flavour as the layers wore off in turn.

We made our selections and watched as they were doled out into small paper bags for the road ahead. The pure secrecy of this mission lent a cachet of independence to our day.

In the winter, the steep slopes of the overpass would turn snowy. One of us would push the other down the side of the overpass and then haul her up by the arm. This usually resulted in the hauler being pulled down and becoming the haulee. After a number of turns of this, one of us—usually me—had to go to the bottom and around to the start of the overpass. We just couldn't scale the steep slippery slope on our own.

Beyond the overpass and Corner Lunch was downtown. The houses were old and didn't all look the same, as they did on our street. People left interesting things on their porches, which were right at the sidewalk, and there was garbage in places it shouldn't be. There was traffic on the streets all the time, and we hurried past Brockville's famous courthouse surrounded by three churches. Then down a short hill to the library.

I loved the Brockville Public Library. It was an old Carnegie library with dark, wood shelves and an ancient grandfather clock. At the desk sat Miss Gilbert with her yellow pencil and metal attachment with the rubber date stamp.

I loved to watch her take out the card from each book, copy my card number on it, and place it carefully aside. Next, she would stamp the return date, two weeks in the future, on a white paper affixed with a gummed label to the inside back cover of the book. Finally, she would stamp my well-weathered junior library card and send us on our way without a smile. For two weeks, I would cherish the books and pore over the dates stamped within my card's tiny boxes, one for each of the six books we could check out at once. The gummed label in the book had a date for every borrower, going back years.

I was also fascinated by the mysterious drawers of cards labelled author, subject, and title. I watched Miss Gilbert slide out the long metal probe that held the cards in the drawer, but they weren't for children to touch.

The children's books were in alphabetical order against the west wall. I would borrow six Dr. Seuss and riddle books for two weeks, though I often would have read them all by the next day. What gets wetter the more it dries? or What has eighteen legs and catches flies? I laughed a lot at those riddles, though not in the library itself.

But at some point, it was time to head back, and, as much I loved books, the highlight of the trip was reserved for the way home.

The Brockville Tabernacle was a small, red-brick building on Buell Street, a few blocks from the library. On our first expedition, we had noticed a white-plastic sign above the door. We could tell that it was lit up at night. We could read the words:

Jesus Saves
Brockville Tabernacle

We had no idea what a modern-day tabernacle was, although the word had come up in Bible readings at the United Church. Why would Jesus choose to save this particular place in a town of so many churches? What would he save it from in a sleepy town like Brockville? Baffled, we did what seven-year-olds do in the face of uncertainty. We made it a joke. We would say it over and over: Jesus saaaaaves the Brockville Tabernacle, Jesus saves the Brockville TABernacle, Jesus saves the BROCKville Tabernacle. And this would lead for some unknown reason to exuberant pushing and shoving and mock sword fights we called "tabernacle fights." And that's how we became tabernacle buddies, though we never set foot inside.

This silliness would last several blocks back to Pearl Street and past the Corner Lunch. By the time we got back to the overpass, we were on to goofy antics like waving or making faces at cars. This would inevitably escalate to theatrics that our parents would never have condoned, like dragging a leg or pretending to limp just to see how people would react. And laughing hysterically. By this point, we would be far past the Godbys' upholstery shop and close to the end of the delicious mile walk back to the suburbs.

* * *

Over the next few years, I was careful to smile with my mouth closed. The crazed grin was gone. My red hair and freckles faded. There was no Janet in the class photo. Sadly, Janet and I were split apart the next year, and for the rest of our school days, by the streaming of the January-to-June children into an accelerated programme. This arbitrary decision left her behind and pushed me forward into the added stress of being both the smallest and the youngest in my class.

Janet was a bright spot in my childhood. She faded in my memories like my red hair, but the joy of our shared laughter remains vivid. Tabernacle fight, anyone?

3 |

My Father's Shop

My father's workshop was a small space, ten by twelve feet, in the basement of our 1950s suburban bungalow. Like my grandfather's full-size, stand-alone outbuilding on his farm, it was always referred to as "the shop," as in "Go down to the shop and get me a hammer."

In the early years, my father's shop had no walls. It was separated on one side from the furnace area, and on the other from our play area, by large shelves made of two-by-fours and plywood. The basement wall formed one end, and the other was open to the laundry area, which at the time had a wringer washer, a double concrete laundry sink, and a floor drain.

The shelves that separated my father's makeshift workspace from the oil tank and furnace were piled with hard-sided leather suitcases, my parents' initials on them in gold letters. Around them were cardboard boxes, many of them empty, stored for future use.

The far wall of the shop was covered by a cupboard my father had built from green treated wood. Its doors opened to expose a treasure trove of tools with coloured handles. There were little shelves and holes for hammers, screw drivers, and a hand drill, as well as drawers that held smaller items. I was amazed that everything had its place, even though it would be decades before I learned the names of all the tools and how to use them.

Up on the side wall, nails, screws, and assorted hardware were visible in small glass jars suspended from four narrow pieces of wood, each with five or six jars. The jar lids had been nailed onto the pieces of wood so that the jars could be easily twisted up into them. This was a common way of storing nails and screws and hooks, but my father had created a mechanism that allowed the rows of jars to rotate. Somehow, the jars were always upright, like seats on a double-wide Ferris wheel. He would spin the rack to find the right jar, creating an almost musical sensation as each row of hardware pieces slid against the glass.

Beside this was the painting area. My father was tidy, but this area was speckled with the paint colours of the rooms and furniture upstairs and the playhouse he had built in the backyard. The shelves here were filled with the materials and tools to putty windows or scrape and sand furniture. My favourite section was the complicated system required to clean paint brushes in the days when all paint was oil-based.

I was fascinated by my father's meticulous system of cleaning brushes with a solvent that came in flat-sided metal gallon cans with a handle and screw top on the upper surface. The solvent was called Varsol or BA Cleaner. It was poured into a tomato can to clean the brushes. The brushes were pumped up and down in the tomato can, and the resulting mixture of cleaner and paint was poured into a big metal container using a paint-stained metal funnel. This was repeated several times with a new batch of Varsol until the solvent was clear. The brushes were then ready to be rubbed with solvent using clean rags from my mother's rag bag (which was actually a box) and hung up to dry.

The cloudy solvent in the big metal container was saved for later. After a few days, the paint settled on the bottom. Then the clear cleaner was decanted into a large glass jar so that it could be reused.

* * *

Next to the paint area, and even more fascinating to me, was a four-by-eight piece of plywood at child-waist height on which my father had mounted my brother's model train set. My father had cut an elliptical hole in the centre of the platform. It was large enough for three children to duck under the plywood and pop up in the middle like groundhogs. The train ran around this hole and had a siding that was controlled by a switch.

I was mesmerized by the switch and by the hum of the train as my brother started it slowly to avoid stalling. Then the train ran round and round, as long as my brother didn't try to speed it up too quickly, in which case it would jump off the track. The engine was maroon and grey in colour like the Canadian Pacific engines that ran on the tracks behind the houses across the street. It smelled like a transistor radio—a warm electric smell—and hummed like a sewing machine as it prepared to move.

* * *

When two more brothers came along, my uncle and my father created a bedroom and rec room in the basement. They closed the shop off, creating a wall outside it for a full-size deep freeze to store vegetables from our garden and a side of beef.

After that, the shop was a dark space out of sight. If we needed a hammer, we had to go in through a door and turn on the shop's only light, a bulb at the ceiling, by pulling a chain. We could no longer glance in on our way to ride our trikes in the open space beyond to see if my father was busy at some small project or to check if the train was set up for a run.

The train set was still on the plywood, but the plywood was now hoisted up against the new permanent wall of the shop. Attached to the wall with hinges, it was pulled up like a drawbridge out of the way. And it rarely came down after that.

My father now parked himself on the couch in the rec room in the evenings. And as I got increasingly distracted by high school activities and music lessons, I stopped going to the basement at all. The light that used to shine from the centre of the basement to the outside walls was now blocked, but my love of tools, paint, and electric trains—and my father—would resurface in the years ahead.

4

The Shoeshine Box

For as long as I can remember, the wooden box sat in our tiny bathroom. It was made of clear pine with a glossy varnish. The back was vertical, but the hinged front angled upwards, meeting a flat top large enough to accommodate a shoe. This rubber surface had small treads where my father could place his foot while he performed his daily shoe-shining ritual.

Inside were the mysteries of shoeshine equipment. The top shelf housed the flat, round tins of shoe polish, each with a small, silver-coloured lever on the side to open the tin and expose the thick, dark, waxy paste. There were three colours: black, brown, and neutral. The bottom shelf held the various brushes and soft, beige cloths that my father used in turn. The white liquid polish he used for my saddle shoes didn't fit in the box, though, and was stored above the toilet along with the cleaning products.

Each morning, after unplugging his electric razor and running a wet brush through his hair, my father's routine was the same. First, he would clean off his teaching shoes, usually the brown ones, with a rough cloth. Next, he applied a base coat of brown polish and allowed it to dry, then buffed it with the soft-bristled brush, whose oval wood handle was a bit larger than his palm. The brush's one-inch brown bristles reminded me of why my father's hairstyle was called a brush-cut.

Then, a second coat of polish and another go at brushing: front, front, front, side, side, side, back, back, back, then repeat. And finally, a top coat of neutral polish—the kind I later used for my own bone-coloured leather shoes—and a final go with the brush. After all this, a gentle buffing with the clean, soft polishing cloth stretched out between his two freckled hands.

I loved the predictability of the process almost as much as I loved my father and the leather shoes he polished so lovingly. I loved the tiny holes and stitching that decorated the leather and that got gummed up with polish if you weren't meticulous enough (this I learned as I got older and was allowed to help). Of the many routines in my life and my father's, this one was the most comforting.

* * *

Almost six decades later, my mother was slowly and painfully downsizing our family home. She would offer up items that she didn't want to discard but didn't want to keep. My brothers and I would send around photos of these items to each other and select those we were willing to take.

My eyes lit up when my mother offered the shoeshine box. I could still see it, tucked between the toilet and the sink, two decades after my father's death.

My niece surprised me by delivering the box to me at our next coffee date. She arrived at the coffee shop with a plastic grocery bag, the shoeshine box inside. She had carried it to work on the bus, and then on the twenty-minute walk from her work to the coffee shop. It wasn't heavy, but it was a bit awkward all the same. As we chatted, I imagined the stand shining in the spacious bathroom of my apartment.

When I got home, tired but happy with expectation, I turned on the foyer light and pulled the box out of its plastic bag. To my chagrin, the shoeshine box was now a far cry from the magical box in my memory. It was now a deep, golden colour of aged pine, scuffed and marred by unidentifiable stains. The rubber tread on the top was still firmly glued in place, but its rich blackness was obscured by a white dust and random blotches of paint in various colours.

The glass knob, which turned out to be hard plastic, had loosened with time. The hinges of the door had broken, and one was missing, so the door hung askew. Inside, the sharp end of a long nail protruded into the bottom shelf, ready to scratch an unsuspecting hand. And the aura of the shoe-shining supplies had vanished. There was not even a lingering smell of shoe polish.

I was astonished by the toll the years had taken on the box. It seems it had not been in the bathroom all these years in homage to my father after all. From the looks of it, someone had used it for a painting project, or maybe it had just been kicking around in the basement storage.

I regretted that my niece had gone to the trouble of bringing it to me—she had even carried it back to my apartment building. I felt sad that reality failed to match my idealized memory of the smell of polish and the feel of soft brown bristles. But I was happy that even in its derelict state, the shoeshine box brought back for a short time the serenity of my father and his shoe-shining ritual.

Pumpkin Head and the Tramp

In the early 1960s, everyone still went out to trick-or-treat, but hardly anyone bought a costume. I liked playing dress-up in my mother's old clothes, but Hallowe'en costumes were torture, especially the masks, which were itchy and confining.

My parents seemed to enjoy creating elaborate costumes though. My father was a drafting teacher who could draw and build anything in 3-D, my mother a former elementary teacher who knew her way around crepe paper. Their handiwork was creative and elaborate, though not always practical.

I envied my brother Robert's ability to pull together a simple and comfortable costume. For several years, he favoured the tramp theme. Robert started with patched clothes and old running shoes. Then he added a cane, my father's old grey fedora, and a mask cut from the back of a cereal box. And away he went. He was well down the street before my parents put the final touches on my costume.

Only two years older than I was, Robert concocted practical costumes that allowed him to run a solo marathon around our local subdivision: thirty-five houses on lower Brookview Crescent and Ferguson Drive, and another fifty up the hill on upper Brookview and Ferguson. Then, after a pit stop to dump his loot, he was off to areas beyond. In later years, he used a pillowcase, which allowed him to collect a lot more candy. It was also less awkward than our paper shopping bags.

Even after trading or discarding the candy he didn't like and bingeing throughout November, he was still digging into his stash of Hallowe'en treats after my carefully managed but smaller take was long gone. One year, he smirked his way to Easter, although the remaining candies were hard, brown molasses kisses that we didn't like.

When I was eight years old, my parents were still making my costumes, but I was old enough to navigate the streets of our small subdivision with my next-door neighbour, Cathy. She was also eight but was six inches taller than I was and already too big for my mother's tiny adult dresses and shoes when we played dress-up.

The most memorable of my parents' creations was made that year: a pumpkin head. My tiny body was comfortably clothed in a light-weight, green sweater that protected me from the chilly night, and I had green pants to match. That was the easy part: the vines.

By contrast, my head was trapped inside an oversized pumpkin—a large, chicken-wire frame, three feet across, covered with orange crepe paper. At the front was a smiling mouth with a hole in it from which my narrow-set eyes could peek out. Above that were pasted-on black, crepe-paper jack-o'-lantern eyes and a green, puffy stem wrapped in more crepe paper.

The pumpkin head was surprisingly light and sat securely on my shoulders. I could see well enough, as long as the ground was flat and I looked straight ahead. Cathy took charge of the screen door, and out we went into the night, each with a paper shopping bag in one hand.

Our street was flat and familiar, but we couldn't hurry due to the awkwardness of my head. Robert was already returning with his first load of candy as we turned the corner and headed up the hill toward upper Brookview. The hill was high enough that my brother could run his go-cart down it, but the slope was gentle enough that I could still see out of my pumpkin's mouth, Cathy faithfully at my side.

We were doing fine, focused but not in a hurry, heading now along the houses on upper Brookview where we didn't know everyone. Our parents trusted us to trick-or-treat pretty much anywhere within walking distance. The reports about razor blades in apples were still in the future. We didn't consider apples a treat anyway, having bushels of them from the local orchard in our cold storage.

Candy apples were a different story. My brother knew which neighbour gave them out and always managed to get there on his first run. He was sure to tell us that he had got one, but we were always too late.

Although we didn't race, we did cut across lawns as much as possible to shorten the distance.

Halfway down upper Brookview, we encountered a small drop-off between one house and the next. It was only a foot high, but my pumpkin head allowed only a view straight ahead, and the streetlights provided little help. Suddenly, the ground in front of me disappeared, and down I went, my candy bag flying, though my head was protected from hitting the ground by the big, chicken-wire pumpkin head.

I was not hurt, but the pumpkin head had taken a beating, and my candy was scattered all over the dark grass. Trapped within the pumpkin head, I was helpless to gather my treats back into my bag. Cathy picked up as much as she could find in the darkness, then handed me my bag as we continued along the street.

Despite the mishap, I was determined to finish going to the remaining houses and return home by the time my brother got back with his third bagful. Robert would not have been deterred by a minor incident like this, I thought. Most likely, he would have whipped off the head and punted it like a football into the shrubbery before continuing on.

On the other hand, you would never have seen my brother wearing a giant pumpkin head to begin with. He would never let himself be constrained by something as cumbersome or ludicrous as this chicken-wire-and-crepe-paper monstrosity.

PRESSURE POINTS

PRESSURE POINTS

There's a Wheel in My Nose

I was nine when my baby brother, Thomas, was born. Most of the time, I enjoyed playing with him, changing him, and feeding him. But I didn't like the responsibility of babysitting him.

By the age of thirteen, I was old enough to stay at home alone and take care of him and my other brother, nine-year-old Richard. I never had problems with them behaving, but I was always afraid of them getting hurt and not knowing what to do.

Like my fellow Girl Guides, I was technically prepared for emergencies and could recite the first-aid procedures needed for badges. However, I would panic under pressure, and my brain would completely shut down. I knew this from other situations like taking tests and feeling faint at the sight of blood.

I was caught off guard one summer evening in our basement rec room when four-year-old Thomas looked up at me and calmly stated, "I've got a wheel in my nose." Even my lively imagination couldn't comprehend what he meant. But sure enough, he had managed to lodge the wheel of a toy car in his nostril.

As I looked more closely, I heard the words "Breathe through your mouth" come out of my own mouth. I looked up the phone number of Mrs. Gifford, the nurse who lived two doors down. Luckily, the telephone book was thin and the numbers were only five digits long. My hands shook as I dialed the number. Even nurse-moms were expected to be at home most of the time.

Mrs. Gifford said, "I'll be right there," but it took an awfully long time for her to arrive. While we waited, I sat with Thomas, saying over and over the only thing I could think of: "Breathe through your mouth." Mrs. Gifford finally arrived. Apparently she had needed to sterilize her tweezers. Our door wasn't locked, and she was able to find us in the rec room.

After skilfully removing the wheel, Mrs. Gifford chatted with us for a few minutes, indulging us with tales of the pencil erasers and other tiny objects she had retrieved from small noses. She said it wasn't a problem, except when the object was a dried pea or bean, which would slowly absorb water.

Luckily the situation was not more serious, and there were no further mishaps. I had functioned under pressure and gotten help. I would never be calm in emergencies, even as an adult, but I had managed. Certainly all one would reasonably expect from a thirteen-year-old bookworm.

Miss Hyde

Lois was an actress and Pam a swimmer, but it was Pam who entertained me most often. We sat together in science class in Grade Eight and when Mr. Gardiner (a.k.a. Daddy Goob) wasn't paying attention, we teased each other and mocked our teachers. Of all the teachers Pam mimicked, Miss Hyde provided the best source material.

Miss Hyde, our homeroom teacher and lover of the classics, delivered a richness of mannerisms. For starters, her diction was second only to her ability to fill the front chalkboard with parsed sentences in perfect schoolteacher handwriting. I loved the organized chaos of the sentences with parts of speech underlined and linked with brackets and arrows.

When Miss Hyde spoke, everyone listened, or at least pretended to. Her deep, manly voice underscored her crisp diction. She would pause dramatically, even when it wasn't necessary, and would gesticulate generously with her hands, a gold signet ring on her pinky.

Our favourite words were *Buddhism* and *longitude*, and we loved to imitate Miss Hyde saying them. First, Pam would pull the hem of her sweater down in a near-perfect Miss Hyde motion. We could almost see Miss Hyde's flat chest and pink sweater set that failed to camouflage the nipples located in the lower regions of her torso.

Her hands still clasping the bottom of her sweater, Pam would purse her lips and make a sound like the French *boude*, her swimmer's diaphragm puffing out a sudden burst of air. And then in contrast, a soft *ism* as if on the inhale. Our first exposure to the concept of Buddhism was overshadowed by the delight of this uncommon and exotic word.

My own favourite was *longitude*, or as Miss Hyde said, *"lonnnnnnnnnn-shitude."* The first syllable, again, accented in her deepest register, her breath flowing through a slightly protruding lower lip. The slightest tremor of her jaw reminiscent of Winston Churchill.

The best part of the longitude parody, and easiest for me to imitate, was that, caught up in her excitement about longitude, her right hand with the pinky ring kept circling an oversize imaginary globe, continuing long after the explanation ended.

This delightfully mockable gesture was surpassed only by Miss Hyde's idiosyncratic idioms, which, unlike *Buddhism* and *longitude*, were repeated week after week. We couldn't wait to hear "Don't split hairs." Its explosive *p* shut down the sibilant *s* and then the testy *t* cut off the lengthy *l*—all in a single word.

I was troubled by another expression: "Don't sit there like a pea on a griddle." As if the imagery wasn't enough, our parody of the sharp, sudden *sit* and the explosion of the *p* became broader and broader as we parroted the expression throughout the year, egged on by its frequent repetition at source.

At the age of twelve, I thought it meant that someone was sitting immobilized and that they should get moving. Finally, in my sixties, I looked it up. It seems that "popping about like a pea on a hot griddle," actually a nineteenth-century expression, means the opposite.

Miss Hyde was a dedicated teacher who, in her excitement about learning, seemed to lose touch with her audience. But she was aware of the class's every movement. Miss Hyde couldn't abide her students wiggling about in their seats like peas on a griddle.

8

Keys to the Car

My father and I were on the way home from my Aunt Marilyn's. She was my father's youngest sister and lived about five blocks from us. We had gone by car, which involved a circuitous route out of our subdivision, past the signal lights of the railroad crossing on Central Avenue, and then down a long street with empty lots and abandoned buildings and into my aunt's subdivision. It was faster to walk there across the railroad tracks, but this was strictly forbidden.

It was late August, and my brother and I had finished the haying at my mother's family farm, and come back home in time for Grandpa Tom's funeral. His youngest and oldest children, my father and Aunt Marilyn, were now working together to settle their father's affairs.

Grandpa Tom, a quiet and resilient farmer, had been diagnosed with a cancer that had spread through his organs. He had died within a few weeks, leaving my father and two aunts to care for my grandmother and the funeral arrangements.

It had been a hard month for my father. Like his father, he could be counted on to take care of things with apparent calm and never showed his emotions. It was not surprising that he had forgotten all about me and my learner's permit, which had been in my wallet since June.

On the day that we visited Aunt Marilyn, my long-awaited sixteenth birthday was two months in the past. In anticipation of driving, I had studied my brother's drivers ed textbook thoroughly. I had walked downtown to the license bureau and passed the test for my learner's permit a few days after my birthday. Then my brother and I had headed off to the farm until we were called back for my grandfather's funeral.

So my father was at the wheel, and I was not thinking about driving. As we passed an old, vacant building, my father suddenly pulled our big red Pontiac Laurentian onto the shoulder of the road. He shut off the car and stated simply, "I guess you want to learn to drive." He got out, came around to the passenger side, and handed me the car keys.

Keys in hand, I hopped into the driver's seat. It didn't require adjustment, as my father was only two inches taller than I was. His confidence in me was much greater than my own, but I was well prepared. In addition to reading the drivers ed book, I had observed my father carefully for many years. Driving a car with an automatic transmission seemed pretty straightforward to me. I had been driving the old Ford tractor for several years, so I even knew about clutches and gears and how to back up, which required turning the steering wheel in a counter-intuitive direction.

What I had somehow missed in all this self-learning was how to turn the car on. The tractor turned on with a push button. Even though I knew where the key went and that I should keep the brake pressed, I was not exactly clear on how to manipulate the key in the starter. After showing me how, my father sat back in the passenger seat to watch me drive the few blocks home. He didn't even put on a seat belt: it wasn't yet mandatory.

Over the next few months, I shadowed my father whenever he went out in the car. A practical person, he later made it clear that we were not to drive around just for fun. He was a "point A to point B" kind of man, so the way to get practice was to drive him wherever he needed to go. Sometimes this meant driving around town taking our family to church or piano lessons. Other times it was highway travel to the school where my father taught in the next town, two exits away on the 401.

I was relieved that my father did not deem it necessary to put a cardboard sign saying "Student Driver" in black crayon on the back of the car as he had with my older brother. My friends had told me about driving around parking lots with their parents. Two of them had damaged their family car by driving off country roads into ditches. My driving was uneventful, my father quietly and calmly beside me, confident that I would learn from experience.

My father believed in learning by doing. We never had to change a tire, but one winter morning, he let me boost the car. He didn't mention that the cables would spark if they touched, and as I watched him prepare the battery, I let the dangling cables collide. Sparks flew with a loud *pop*! He was right. I learned quickly not to do that again.

My father also believed in rewarding our competence and responsibility.

On cold winter days, he had a system to warm up the car before he headed out to work. In addition to the block heater, he had installed a small Torcan heater that warmed the inside of the car. When he came home after work, he would plug the car into the socket beside the driveway. Then in the morning, he would flip a switch on the basement stairway to turn on the power. By the time he had dressed and eaten breakfast, the chill was off the car's interior and the windshield was easy to clean.

When my brother and I started taking the car out in the evenings, it was up to us to plug in the car so it would be warm in the morning.

I am not sure how my brother did in this regard, but I was diligent, pushing both plugs deep into the cold-hardened extension cord. Unfortunately, I didn't quite understand the concept of waiting until morning to flip the switch on. My father stifled a smile the next day when he gently informed us that the power had been on all night. It seems that after eight hours of heating, the car was toasty. Even the back window of the huge Pontiac was crystal clear that morning!

Our other responsibility was to put the key back when we returned the car. The key hung beside the stairs at the back door. This was my father's final test for us. Could we remember to return it every single time?

I passed this test, too. On Valentine's Day, less than six months after the day my father first handed me his car keys, I came home to an envelope on my bed. It was particularly memorable because my father wasn't inclined to give us cards or presents, and the greeting card was designed for a six-year old. It was shaped like a pink lamb, with a surprising text: "You are such a dear little miss."

Inside, the printed text obviously ended with the final rhyming word, "kiss," but my father had covered the word with a folded piece of paper. On it, he had penned in uppercase: "THIS." With great anticipation, I opened up the little piece of paper which revealed, to my delight, my very own key to the family car.

9

The Brown Paper Bag

I had almost finished high school when two unexpected things happened to enrich my life. The first was the appearance of someone new in our church's youth group. The second was a phone call from a neighbour asking if I would be interested in a part-time job at the local pharmacy. These changes, welcome and exciting in my monotonous world, ended up colliding unexpectedly.

The new youth-group member, who shall remain nameless, was a playful and quirky character. He was in the grade ahead of me, but we had a common spare period. We sat together in the library to study, but often socialized instead.

We chatted each day at school over the crossword puzzle during our spare. We met up on Sunday nights for youth-group activities: square dancing and singing popular songs such as Don McLean's "American Pie." I even joined the track team so we could both run the halls after school.

We laughed a lot, which was refreshing for me. His dark hair, a tad shorter than the 1970s shoulder-length style, was parted ironically in the centre. He had replaced his square, horn-rimmed glasses, always taped up from basketball incidents, with round wire frames more evocative of Groucho Marx than John Lennon. He had a *hyuck hyuck* laugh and bizarre antics like making butterflies from Kleenex tissues.

He became my square-dance partner, maybe because we were the oldest members of the group, but that didn't matter to me. Square dancing was, like his haircut, ironic. It was fun to be together, to be holding hands, to be goofing around. It was all such innocent fun, with no pressure.

After he left for university, my drugstore job took over as I padded my bank account for my own departure the following year. In addition to the rather generous pay, $1.95 per hour, I was treated like an adult, a real staff member, though I was not yet eighteen.

At first, I spent my time at the mindless but enjoyable task of emptying cardboard boxes of shampoo and deodorant, using a ticket gun to tag them with a date and price. It seemed like a simple task.

On my first day, I was filling several shelves on an end display unit with large bottles of Scope mouthwash. Suddenly, the whole shelf collapsed, taking the lower one with it. I was surrounded by a puddle of foul-smelling, green liquid and open-mouthed customers coming in the door behind me.

What a surprise when Cal, the soft-spoken store manager, came over and apologized to me! He hadn't secured the shelves properly, he admitted. He called the cleaner over, and that was that. No fuss, no muss.

A further kindness came from Mrs. Wilson, who managed the cosmetics counter. She had well-tanned skin, a husky laugh, and a compassionate smile. We chatted from time to time, and then she started to offer me perfume samples.

She and my mother were in the same rug-hooking class, and she knew enough not to send me home dolled up with mascara and eye shadow. But she was an ace at saving perfume testers for me. My growing shelf of scents became my girl-signature: Charlie, Love's Baby Soft, Wild Musk Oil, and my favourite, a deep earthy scent called Ambergris that came in a dark-green cylinder with a round-tipped dabber. I became a perfume junkie that year, completely oblivious to the advertising tag lines for these products: "Because innocence is sexier than you think."

As I grew more competent and confident, I learned to operate the cash register on the weekends and evenings when the regular staff were off. I had practiced making change at home, but I wasn't expecting the cash register to have a row of buttons on the right side. These were labelled with various departments such as pharmacy, paper products, and cigarettes (these were prominently displayed in regular or king-size behind me). We had to select a department because some products were taxable. In fact, the machine could only tally the items if you chose one of these buttons.

It seemed complicated at first, and, like all new pressures, it made me nervous and awkward. Once I got the hang of it, though, I calmed down. There were busy periods, but mostly it was a relaxing job among the pleasant smells of paper products and soaps. There were other store staff to help if I needed them, and I didn't have to balance cash at the end of the day. The customers were usually friendly, and I recognized a lot of them.

Late one afternoon, I looked up from my cash and watched two people approaching: a man in his forties followed by a younger man about half his age. The young man had centre-parted dark hair and John Lennon glasses. Yes, it was my quirky and ironic friend. I was a bit nervous. I hadn't seen him since he left for university.

The older man—I guessed he was an uncle—came up to the cash, with my friend slightly behind and looking down at the floor. The uncle had in his hand a small paper bag that looked like a pharmacy bag, but brown, not white. He placed the bag on the counter and said distinctly, "Twenty-five cents." OK, I thought, seeing that there was no sticker or writing. I couldn't think of a reason for him to be telling a lie.

But I did need to know which department to put it in. After all, I couldn't ring it up without a category, could I? Reaching towards the bag to check inside, I was brusquely brushed aside by the uncle.

I stammered, "I, I need to know what it is."

"It's from the pharmacy."

That's all I really needed. I focused on the cash register to avoid seeing my friend's face, bereft of its trademark quirky grin.

For weeks after the event, I played scenarios in my mind. Was the uncle a con man, trying to rip off something more expensive? Had he persuaded the pharmacist to open a box of individual items so he could purchase only one? Was my friend an accomplice or an unwitting diversion?

A month or two later, I was watching two boys shopping for condoms in the movie *Summer of '42*, and I suddenly wondered if the uncle had been welcoming my innocent friend into manhood, though in a way that was sure to embarrass him.

I wonder what the situation looked like from the other point of view. If you recognize yourself, old friend of mine, please let me know. I'd love to see that grin again.

10

I Am Not You

I didn't spend much time in the summer with my friends. While Cathy and Shelley were at their cottages and Pam was lifeguarding at the city pool, I was away at the farm with my grandparents. So it was a rare occasion to be at Shelley's cottage on Charleston Lake one summer afternoon. It was a glorious day, and we were now old enough to drive ourselves.

Things were fine until someone suggested that we swim across the bay, about one hundred metres across. The day wasn't particularly windy, but the size of the lake meant that there were always waves. For Cathy, Shelley, and Pam, this was a breeze, given the amount of time they spent swimming.

The very idea of being out from shore struck terror in my heart: I couldn't swim. More precisely, I took lessons as a child, but never really lost my fear of the water. Nervous thrashing was the best I could do. I didn't even know how to breaststroke.

Feeling pressured to swim with my friends across the open water, I was aware there were few cottages and no adults close by. I protested without success. Of course I could swim that far, my friends scoffed! They made it clear that they were going, and I didn't want to be left behind.

Reluctantly, I rationalized that Pam was a lifeguard, and I allowed myself the folly of setting out with them. I made the best of things and pretended to be someone I was not. I took the chance that my will alone could get me across the bay.

I was still managing to swim at the halfway point. The fear of the open water was outpaced by the sheer determination and physical effort required to keep going. The thought of being left behind loomed as we crawled towards the far shore. I was breathing hard, but I was doing it.

As Pam started her final sprint, my friends followed her lead, and I was indeed left far behind, flagging. The other shore of the bay seemed an eternity away. And then it happened. I ran out of steam, out of breath, took in water, and started to panic. What if I yelled and they didn't hear me?

I flailed about, and luckily Pam was somehow alerted to my distress. She swam back strongly and with confidence, as I knew she would. She forced me on my back and grabbed me around the neck as she had been trained. She towed me what seemed like another hundred metres to safety.

Safe on the rock at last, Pam chastised me in a voice borrowed from a finger-wagging great-aunt. I fought her, she said, and wouldn't let her turn me over to be towed. As if I didn't feel bad enough already! I had failed to swim. I had failed to convince my friends I couldn't swim. I had even failed to be a cooperative person to rescue! And we still needed to get back to the cottage somehow.

As Pam and I inched around the edge of the lake through the underbrush of the Scout camp, my feelings of emotional distress outweighed the physical discomfort of scratchy bushes and stones on bare feet. I was just too embarrassed to feel relieved.

But Pam had saved my life, and now she was the one guiding me around the bay while the others swam back across its shiny waters.

FRESH AIR

FRESH AIR

11

Making Hay While the Sun Shines, Part 1

When my older brother, Robert, and I were twelve and ten, the arrival of a letter in my grandfather's handwriting took us by surprise. Could we come help with the haying? My mother's father, now in his early sixties, had given up the dairy cattle and pigs that had been his livelihood. His current herd of twenty Black Angus beef cattle didn't need to be milked twice a day, but he and my grandmother were still bringing in enough hay and grain from the farm fields to feed them.

Now my grandmother, increasingly "crippled up" by rheumatism, was finding it too hard to drive the tractor. My brother and I leapt at the chance to get away from our suburban bungalow, our parents, and our little brothers.

Our job each afternoon was to tromp on the hay that my grandfather threw forward into the hay wagon. He was still using a traditional hay loader that was pulled behind a wagon, until recently by horses. Minnie and May, two Clydesdales with long, white hair on their ankles, had pulled this wagon and loader for many years with no need for hydraulics or fossil fuel.

Now the tractor pulled the wagon along the windrows of hay that had been raked up and dried. Attached behind the wagon, the hay loader picked up the loose hay. Its two oversize metal wheels drove a flat chain, which in turn created an alternating movement of long strips of wood with metal picks. The picks pulled the hay up the slippery slope to the wagon.

The hay then dropped ten feet into the wagon past my grandfather's head. It kept coming steadily as the tractor and wagon proceeded slowly down the field and had to be spread around in the wagon. My grandfather, with my brother's help, would heft the loose hay with a three-tined hay fork into the front of the wagon. My brother and I took turns tromping it down.

Over the next years, my grandfather's confidence in my brother and me grew. We took turns driving the grey Ford tractor. If the weather was good this would take most of July, working steadily from one o'clock until supper at six. We worked six days a week. Sundays were reserved for church and resting up.

Robert and I were very familiar with the Ford tractor. Both our grandfathers had the same model. Symmetrical, compact, and solid, the Ford had two large, grey fenders that looked like elephant ears over the huge rear tires. The fenders were a perfect sitting place for kids, tiny bums pressed against the fenders and feet on the rust-brown housing that covered the axle below.

At the back of the tractor, a horizontal drawbar half-way to the ground provided a handy step up. My brother preferred to scramble up the front of the thick raised treads of the tires, one hand pulling on the steering wheel.

The Ford tractor was an excellent design for small people like my brother and me to drive. We could use our full force by standing on the clutch and, if needed, the brake. Unlike my grandfather's older tractor, a red Farmall Cub that always seemed about to tip over, the Ford tractor was easy to drive. My grandfather had already started it by pushing the round button. *Chug chug chug rooooom*! All we had to do was to put it in first gear by standing on the clutch, manipulating the gear stick over and up into first, and slowing letting up on the clutch.

The haying operation proceeded down the field at a pace so slow that a toddler could have kept up. The tractor was so steady on the flat field that it could almost have followed the windrows all by itself. There was little to do except keep an eye out for oversized groundhog holes, which would jostle the tractor, and the whole load.

In the twenty-acre field, the corners were infrequent and wide. I could sit for the length of a city block with absolutely no distractions, pondering the old apple trees along the edges of the field. I was fascinated by the rocky foundations where the house used to sit. My grandfather often talked about his parents moving the house to where it was now, close to the blacktop road. They had moved it on a sleigh with horses.

Sitting on the wide seat of the tractor, I could sing at the top of my lungs and no one could hear me over the noise of the engine. I loved driving the tractor, while my brother enjoyed the extreme physical exertion and satisfaction of piling and tromping hay until there was so much hay in the wagon that it was nearly falling off the sides.

When it was time to head back to the barn, my grandfather drove the tractor. My brother and I perched on the elephant-ear fenders beside him. We preferred this to the more exciting but more childlike ride atop the hay wagon. The noise of the tractor didn't allow for conversation, so I had plenty of time to observe the horizontal crevices of my grandfather's brown, sun-baked neck, exposed between his green cotton cap and the frayed collar of his sweat-soaked farmer shirt.

My brother and I started off wearing thin, white, body-hugging T-shirts, shorts, and running shoes in the summer heat. We soon learned why my grandfather wore heavy cotton pants, wool socks, and work boots. The hay was quite prickly, and we ended up red and itchy all over our legs.

My grandmother let us learn this the hard way but insisted that we wear hats. She provided me with a shapeless red-felt hat, which was hot but good protection for my fair skin. My brother dug up an old straw boater with a fading blue band bearing the words "Brockville Summer Carnival."

The drive back to the barn was a faster and bumpier ride. The tractor was now in second gear, and we quickly got to the edge of the field and across the small ditch that was a raging creek in springtime but barely a trickle by summer. My grandfather had constructed a temporary bridge halfway down the side of this four-foot drop, so driving the tractor with its now towering and tippy load of hay across was an adventure.

First, my grandfather would put the tractor back into first gear and start down the forty-five-degree slope towards the bridge on two narrow paths worn by the tractor tires. At this point, the wagon behind was on the level field. The weight of the wagon and hay down onto the bridge was counteracted by the pull of the tractor's steady engine in first gear.

Then, as the tractor got down to the level wooden planks of the bridge at the bottom of the slope, my grandfather would gun the engine using a sun-faded silver lever. The ascent up the other side required a sudden and considerable burst of power to get the load up to the level field without stalling. I held my breath in anticipation every time my grandfather accomplished this feat.

We always got up the other side without incident and passed through a smaller hayfield that sloped up to the house and drive shed. We proceeded up the hill on the main lane that led from the back pasture to the barn. This path was wider, with fences on both sides. It was well worn and not quite straight due to rocks jutting through the soil here and there.

On the way up the hill to the barn, it was our job to jump down and open and close the gates so the cattle wouldn't end up in the hayfields. My grandfather worried that they would eat too much and get bloated, though I was not sure what that meant. My brother almost always jumped down first, although sometimes I joined him and walked the rest of the short way up to the barn.

12

Making Hay While the Sun Shines, Part 2

The doors at the back of the barn were about fifteen feet high and nearly as wide to accommodate the hay wagon and, later in the season, the mill used to thresh the grain. Sometimes we had to open the barn doors by rotating a big weathered one-by-ten board, which swung round on an oversized nail in the middle.

This board was barely within my reach, especially if it had been left horizontal instead of at a downward angle. When we were younger and couldn't reach the board, we would crawl into the barn through a rough-edged hole that allowed the dogs and cats to enter freely.

The most impressive of my grandfather's tasks was backing the load of hay up into the barn.

First, he drove it up a steep slope in well-worn, stony ruts and onto a flat area behind the barn. This plateau had barely enough room to manoeuvre the wagon and tractor. It was surrounded on one end by the barn, on one side by a shed, and on the other side by a rocky slope that led down to the front of the barn. At the far end there was a steep, rocky drop-off to the pasture below.

My grandfather drove towards this drop-off, then pivoted the back end of the massive load towards the barn. My brother and I stood guard, giving signals if the wagon was too far to one side or the other, as the Ford tractor pushed it slowly back and up onto the well-worn boards of the barn floor. My grandfather turned off the tractor and put blocks of wood behind the tires. We were ready for the next step of the operation.

If it was really hot, my grandfather sometimes took a short break to go up the hill to the outdoor well where he had a cup or two of water from the communal tin mug hanging there on a hook. On "good drying days," as he called fair days with low humidity and a brisk breeze, he was rested enough and cooled down from the drive. The sweat of his soaking shirt had evaporated, leaving salty, white stains.

Next the hay was moved from the wagon into the haymow (which he pronounced to rhyme with *cow*). My brother would thrust a black, C-shaped, cast-iron fork—half as tall as he was and almost as heavy—into the hay. The fork lifted a pile of hay up past the rafters and then traveled the length of two large houses to the far end of the barn using an elaborate system of coconut-fibre ropes and pulleys.

I sat up on the flat granary roof beside the wagon, listening for the sound of my grandfather's booming voice from the far end of the mow, made faint by distance and increasing quantities of hay: "TRIP IT!" The timing of this was sometimes critical if my grandfather had decided to swing the load to one side to avoid heaving the hay so far by hand. When we tripped the big heavy fork by pulling hard on another rope, the pile of hay would fall from the rafters and land with a dull *thud* and *swoosh* of dust in the mow where my grandfather was waiting. There, he would again lift each pile of hay with his three-tined fork and spread it evenly across the mow.

When the wagon was empty, we took a break. We drank more water from the tin cup and sat on the front verandah. My grandfather smoked a cigarette, hand-rolled in thin, white paper from a bright yellow folder with a lady on it. Then back we went for another load. This was making hay while the sun shines, as my grandmother would say.

After several loads, my grandfather would check his pocket watch. If it was close to six, the last load of hay had been brought in for the day. We then closed the barn doors and headed up to the house for supper.

My grandmother was keeping one eye on the kettle and the other on the size of the load that determined the timing of our return. She had supper on the table—a light meal of cold meat and garden-fresh vegetables. We had eaten our dinner, a big meal of meat and potatoes, at noon. My grandfather finished off his supper with a large chunk of orange cheddar from the cube-shaped glass cheese dish. After we ate, Percy Saltzman on CBC drew the weather forecast on his chalkboard, tossed his chalk into the air, and caught it.

Our final chore was to help dry the dishes, and then my brother and I were free for the evening. We would sit on the front verandah with my grandfather, petting the barn cats or watching them evade the barn swallows that tormented them. The swallows had the nasty habit of dive-bombing us too. We waved at the odd car that passed by. My grandfather would make a grunting noise that sounded something like *uhlo* even though he knew they couldn't hear him.

On nights when my grandfather wasn't too tired, he would tell us stories about when he was younger or about his family, who had come over from Ireland and lived for four generations on this same family farm. Other times I sat by myself, waiting for a car to break the monotony. The sounds of the ball game or the Irish Rovers came through the screen door of the country kitchen.

In the morning, my grandfather was up at 5:30 a.m. to do chores before making his boiled egg in a small metal pot lined with white lime residue from the well water. My brother was right behind, shadowing my grandfather as he greased and fixed the machinery or checked out the cattle. In the late morning, they cut hay with a mower on the little Cub tractor and raked the previous day's cut into windrows to dry. There were unlimited tasks to keep my brother busy, sometimes back in the fields and sometimes in the cool downstairs of the barn or the workshop out behind the house.

My grandmother and I stayed in bed until close to 9:30 a.m., and, in those early years, I was mostly free to read or write stories in left-over school notebooks until it was time to get dinner on the table for noon on the dot, listen to the weather, and have a short nap. Then, as long as the sun shone, we were back in the hayfield again.

13

The Pink Paint

My grandmother was fixing up the bedroom at the top of stairs. Or rather, she was planning, and my parents and I were fixing. I slept in this long, narrow room when I was at the farm in the summers, and now that I was a teenager, I was involved in the process of updating the room and the furniture.

My father, free of summer school, was staying with my mother and younger brothers in our house trailer at the lake nearby. Urged on by my mother, he was working through her parents' four bedrooms upstairs in the aging frame house. My grandmother's health, and consequently the house, had been deteriorating for years, although she was only in her early seventies.

Like the other bedrooms, mine had layers of flowered wallpaper that had accumulated on the crumbling horsehair plaster. The closet was an old pole in the corner.

The bed was a hollow metal frame with heavy springs and a real feather tick. My grandmother was no longer able to knead the tick into shape and planned to replace it with a regular spring mattress. How I would miss snuggling into that nest of feathers!

While my father built a new closet with a shelf and accordion doors with gold-coloured handles, my mother hauled several large wallpaper books home from the paint store in town.

My grandmother narrowed the choices to two, one a traditional floral pattern that seemed to match my grandmother's elegant and traditional taste. This was my preference, too, although I could see how matching the flowers would be challenging. The second pattern was abstract and 1970s and very, very pink.

I hated the pattern, and I hated pink, but the decision was not mine to make. This I had learned years earlier when the deep blue-green I wanted for our family car was overruled and we ended up with the popular light-blue model. My disappointment outlived both the car and the wallpaper.

I didn't get to choose the colour or pattern, but I did get to help with the painting and papering. It was an art to get the wallpaper straight and to match the wet strips without wastage. This was even harder on the slanted wall. The house was over a century old, so the walls were not neat and flush, despite my father's best efforts to patch them.

My father showed me to how to cover the white baseboards with oil-based paint, massaging the woodwork with brushstrokes to spread a thin but thorough coat of paint. By the time I finished, I felt like an expert.

After the room was papered and my parents left, my grand-mother and I turned to the furniture. She decided we would spruce up a light-green wood bedframe and dresser to match—and tone down—the wallpaper. My grandmother was a strong advocate of re-painting in the same colour to avoid embarrassing paint chips, so the bed would remain green. The headboard had a few simple grooves in the shape of flower petals and the dresser a few swirls of molding. These would remain pink.

At my grandmother's suggestion, I salvaged a sap bucket from the mouse-ridden loft over the drive shed and proceeded to sand off the rust. I was to paint it the same green, with pink inside. My grandmother would cut a pink rose from her stash of old greeting cards. Voilà, a custom wastepaper basket.

My grandmother's plan in place, it was time to purchase the paint. We would need a quart of green paint and a tiny tin of pink from the hardware store in town. My grandfather and I were to handle the purchase. My grandmother had not left the house in close to a decade, except for a rare visit to the chiropractor and, later, for my wedding at the local church.

I was used to my grandfather delegating small errands. He had been showing my brother and me how to compare prices on various sizes of food for many years. He would hand us the purse, as he called his leather wallet, to buy my grandmother's favourite sticky, pecan- and cherry-laden Chelsea buns at the bakery.

The day we set out for paint, my grandfather stayed in the car. My brother was now working in the city and preparing for university, so I was on my own, the purse in one hand, wallpaper sample in the other. I was always nervous in new situations, but never dared to say no. Once inside the store, I cautiously approached the clerk and explained what I needed.

The green paint, he said, was easy, as he set up the paint-mixing machine. The pink paint, in a small tin, was a problem. They didn't have any pink in small tins, he said. He would need to mix up a quart of paint.

I was stuck. My grandmother needed the paint, and this was the only option. It never occurred to me to go out to the car and ask my grandfather what to do. Dutifully, I bought the paint, and an hour later I was sitting at the harvest table in the country kitchen.

My grandmother tried her best to camouflage her distress about the huge can of pink paint. She was silent about my mistake, although her grey eyes said it all. It was one thing that the cost seemed enormous among their frugal expenditures. But what on earth would we do with a quart of pink paint? Still, she was not inclined to make me feel ashamed, since I had done my best.

I stayed a few summers in the ghastly pink-wallpapered room with the green and bubble-gum-pink furniture before going off to university.

* * *

A decade passed, and I was married with two young children. We visited my grandmother every week or two, and now she was asking me to help clean up the shelves on the stairs leading to the basement.

I had passed down these stairs many times to seek out jars of preserves in the dark, dirt-floored basement with a huge cement water cistern. I hadn't paid much attention to the paints that sat on the cobweb-laden shelves on the way down.

Now I was confronted with an archive of paint cans that I remembered and others that were even older. I recognized a small tin of silver rust paint that I had used for the mailbox and the water heater, a quart can almost full of blue paint matching the big country kitchen, and of course, a quart of pink-bubble-gum-coloured paint.

At my grandmother's request, I boxed up all the paints and took them home. A few of them I discarded, as they were dried up and beyond salvaging. I used the blue paint to refresh my picnic table, regretting it when the blue paint chipped off to reveal patches of dark green. As usual, my grandmother was right.

I didn't always follow my grandmother's advice, but I did adopt her deep-seated need to economize and not waste. And I still felt a bit guilty about that pink paint.

And that is how my daughters came to have a pink bedroom. Not the walls! No, I used up the pink paint, which they did like (at least I think they did). I repurposed several old pieces of furniture that we had accumulated from various rental houses—a dresser, bed frame, and a piece of plywood—to create a loft bed for two. And I painted it all pink.

Over the years, I came up with many variations of furniture with found objects, and my daughters carried on this tradition when they got their own apartments. My grandparents, like many of their generation, were masters at making something from nothing. In the early years, when I wasn't working, this was a necessity for my young family. Unable to afford showroom furniture, I covered up my shame with a competence bordering on false pride, cobbling together a home for my children from scraps of this and that.

After my grandparents left the farm, the green bed and dresser with the pink trim came to our basement along with many other memories of my grandparents. My daughter Abby claimed the sap-bucket wastepaper basket, with the rose on the side and pink interior, for her bedroom.

Almost three decades later, it was among the few items that she requested when I downsized and sold our family home.

Trashy Reading Material

My grandfather and I were headed up the blacktop road towards the dump. We were blasting along on the Ford tractor in fourth gear. While slow for a car, the speed was exhilarating compared with the snail's pace of first gear in which we plodded through the hayfields.

The township dump—which we called the Drummond Township Trading Post—was fairly new. Until recently, farmers along the road had mostly burned or buried their garbage. Large hulks of rusting machinery and cars graced the edges of the fields and bush lots. Whether to meet the needs of city slickers moving out to the area or government regulations, the dump had become the place where garbage was burned communally. As a result, an odious black cloud now wafted over the adjacent farms.

On the upside, the dump had an unspoken rule that anything remotely salvageable could be left beside the road that surrounded the dump, safe from the smelly mess of waste smouldering in the pit below. Along the curved and rutted road around the dump was a veritable bazaar of treasures, from folding lawn chairs in need of webbing (my father's specialty) to old furniture and appliances.

But this day, the treasure was not at the dump, it was in the ditch on the way there.

We were just starting off down the road, just out of sight of my grandmother standing on the porch, when my grandfather stopped the tractor and jumped down, spying something in the ditch. It was a damp but intact paperback, close to two inches thick.

"Here's a book for you! I don't have me glasses."

My grandfather's seventy-year-old eyes were still sharp, though he now needed reading glasses. He handed the book up to me, perched on the giant elephant ear fenders that served as passenger seating. My grandfather revved the tractor up, and we were off again. The title didn't seem important to him. It was a book, so it was a treasure.

*　*　*

The rest of the trip was uneventful and passed quickly while I pondered how to sneak the book inside before my sharp-eyed grandmother could notice. When we arrived back at the farm, I ran ahead into the house and upstairs while my grandfather took the tractor to the drive shed. He was barely in the house when he told my grandmother about the find with the excitement of a child. I carefully suppressed any incriminating details about the title and content.

I found some coloured newsprint from the weekend section of an old *Ottawa Journal* in the box beside the woodstove. I was quite skilled at making book covers, having eight years of experience covering school textbooks. Although I was rusty, now being in high school, I accomplished a tidy but nondescript cover and tucked the book away to read later.

During the long summers on the farm, I had been reading novels purchased for my mother's high school classes. They were housed in a wooden orange crate that served as a stand for an old coal-oil lamp. A cotton curtain, dark green with a flower pattern, hung from a thick cord, keeping the dust off them. I read my way through books from *Jane Eyre* to *Cheaper by the Dozen* with the help of a small, leather-covered dictionary.

My grandfather's present, though, was a new genre to me. For several days, I found quiet moments in my bedroom to complete it, stashing it out of sight between readings. At the end of the summer, I took it back home, and it ended up in the trunk of possessions that I took to university.

I don't recollect the content, but the title is still emblazoned in my memory: *Grandpa Likes 'em Young.*

15

Darn Those Socks

My father was great at fixing things. He could repair lamps. He could repair china knickknacks broken by kids. He could repair holes in socks—using hockey tape. My grandmother told me about her son-in-law's socks over and over, chuckling to herself.

Over the years, she benefited from my father's generosity and competence with small repairs and fixing the old horsehair plaster upstairs. I dare say she came to appreciate and respect him. But when she first met him, the hockey tape on his socks shocked and bothered her. What kind of person had her only daughter married?

As luck would have it, my grandmother loved to darn socks. She never liked to sew, although she had a heavy, black Singer sewing machine, a modern electric one that had replaced her old treadle model. She used it for functional tasks like mending my grandfather's green work pants and for braided-rag rugs to keep outside dirt off the floors.

In the evenings, she didn't knit or crochet or do stitching. She preferred playing solitaire or reading the newspaper or the purple-covered prayer book with its flowing King James language. Or darning socks.

As a farmer, my grandfather wore through a lot of thick, wool work socks. It amazed me that he would wear what seemed like winter socks in the hot summer. I learned later, when tree planting, that they were just the thing to absorb and wick moisture. My grandfather's socks were washed in the old wringer washer and stretched onto wood or metal stretchers to dry by the wood stove.

I remember my grandmother sitting in her wooden rocker, which my father later repaired and refinished. She would pull out a rounded ball with a handle. I learned recently that these are called "darning mushrooms" and date back centuries. The one my grandmother used was a work of art. Its smooth wood was varnished to highlight the contrasting grains and colours of the wood. It reminded me of the lamps and furniture my father had made with care and attention to detail in his woodworking shop. I suspect he made it for my grandmother.

My grandmother would pull out long strands of wool—usually grey to match my grandfather's socks—and weave them lovingly across the hole in the sock, back and forth, up and down, like a hand-woven mini-blanket. I tried to imitate her technique: straight, tight stitches that melded into a soft surface after a few washes.

Well into her eighties, my grandmother was still darning socks. It was a labour of love, something she enjoyed. My grandfather was now renting out the farm fields, and my father had slowed down after hip surgeries. My brother Robert, still energetic and helpful, remained a faithful provider of worn socks and a worthy recipient of her quiet affection.

ENCHANTMENT AND DISENCHANTMENT

ENCHANTMENT AND DISENCHANTMENT

16

The Yellow Room

My first daughter, Charlotte, was just past her first birthday when we moved into a rented house on Gladstone Avenue. This was our third rental in central Ottawa and the first right downtown. We could walk to the library and museums in a few minutes.

I was pregnant, and we were ecstatic to have a three-bedroom house. We wouldn't have to lug a stroller up and down cement stairs like we did at our house high above Loretta Avenue. And there was so much room.

The house on Gladstone had been rented by a rolling roster of co-op students. When we moved there, the two walls of cupboards in the kitchen were so full that we thought the tenants had not moved out. Our first months at the house became an ongoing, free yard sale, as we moved anything we didn't want out onto the narrow strip of grass that served as a front lawn.

Adult faces would appear in the windows of the apartments across the street, above the shop that sold rubber stamps. A few minutes later, small children would run across the busy street to pick up the treasures: toys and kitchen implements and small furniture.

There was a country kitchen at the back, which made this a mansion compared to our previous house. We now had plenty of room for a full-size washer right in the kitchen, and our freezer no longer had to be stuffed in the hallway.

The most luxurious part of the house, though, was above the country kitchen. It was an oversize bedroom at the top of the stairs leading from the front door. When it was warm, and the noise and the fumes from the paint shop across the street weren't blowing our way, we could leave the inside front door open to get extra light.

The small window on the south side of the bedroom overlooked the backyard and the houses behind on McLeod Street. It was perfect for a toddler to look out: extra low and small because the addition had been built with a pitched roof. The room had not one, but two slanted ceilings. Best of all, someone had painted the walls and ceiling a sunflower yellow and had left a bright-red carpet that covered most of the painted plywood floor.

We had lots of space for boxes, toys, and extra clothing for the new baby who would arrive in November, and I created a small corner for my desk and sewing machine. I had traded in the basic Singer that my parents had bought me as a wedding present and was now using a new model that could sew the stretchy fabrics that had become so popular in the late 1970s.

Having my own sewing machine for the past five years had allowed me to experiment. I had graduated from sewing skirts and tops to more complex and adventurous items like a winter coat with wool and chamois linings. While pregnant with Charlotte, I had branched out even further to larger projects for our previous rental: bedspreads, curtains, and plastic crib accessories.

Now I was back to clothing, but mostly for children. I spent hours on appliquéd clothing for Charlotte and her cousin, who was the same age. My favourite project was two sets of overalls, one with a dog and the other with a lion, their tails extending up over the shoulder strap. Later, I would make smocked pinafores for both my daughters and a younger cousin. They were a far cry from the beautiful smocked dresses my mother had made for me, but they provided me with a challenge and a sense of accomplishment during the diaper-filled days ahead.

Another advantage of the yellow room's ample space was a rack and pull-out cord clothesline to dry frozen clothes and diapers from the outside line on short winter days. The smell of outdoors, including a neighbour's wood stove, added to the ambiance of happy mornings before our long afternoon naps.

Before Abby was born, Charlotte and I spent many happy days together in silence, each in our own world. Although there was lots of room to play, Charlotte's favoured spot was a couple of feet from me on the red carpet while I sewed.

Charlotte would sit with a book for hours, even though she wasn't yet two. One of her favourites, left by previous tenants, was an alphabet book with pop-ups, some of which were held up by small wires. I wasn't concerned about Charlotte damaging the book, nor was I concerned about the book's wires hurting her. I just didn't worry much in those days, and Charlotte seemed more careful than other toddlers. Like me, it was her mind that provided adventure.

Our parallel play in the yellow room was quiet and companionable. I would miss this calm activity when the new baby came. Having two children would be very different from having one!

17

Barbie Bubbling Spa

"It's a Barbie Bubbling Spa!" Charlotte was holding the box in front of her. The box, nearly as big as her torso, was bright pink like the plastic toy revealed through its cellophane window. As she shook the box up and down, up and down again, I could see Charlotte's eyebrows raised with delight, and then, as the box covered her face, her pilled, polyester housecoat, hastily thrown on against the cold, came into view.

Charlotte had talked non-stop for months about this toy she had been seeing on television. I was regretting our decision to let our children watch TV after many years of resisting. In those days before VCRs, we were victim to commercials that couldn't be skipped, especially during the months before Christmas.

My daughters' exposure to consumerism had been limited to hearing the promotion of the toys of the year by their TV-watching cousins and friends: Cabbage Patch Kids dolls, Wrinkles, and Care Bears. Somehow my brothers or friends, who had professional jobs, always came through with one of those must-have toys for them.

As for presents from their parents, my children had lower expectations. They did have me, a full-time mom at home who took them to free museums and baked healthy cookies. But there was no money for extras such as store-bought clothes and pricey toys. Luckily, their friends at our community school shared our low income level, so I didn't feel pressured to buy popular toys and name brands.

The year of the bubbling spa, I was quite aware that Santa wouldn't be coming to our house much longer, and my children would soon be more worldly and critical. So, I splurged on brand-new toy for each of them.

Charlotte's obsession with the bubbling spa made it easy. Abby, two years younger, was easily satisfied. She had circled every item in the Sears Wish Book that year, still happy with anything Santa decided to bring. Warm in her fuzzy yellow onesie, she was thumping up a storm on a shiny white toy piano with tall legs and a red plastic bench.

These two toys, at twenty dollars each, were a big purchase. Normally this would have been the budget for all their presents, which would typically include used toys discovered at the Neighbourhood Services second-hand shop and scrubbed clean. I would make games and purchase small trinkets from the Giant Tiger discount store up the street. Their stockings were filled with miniature cereal boxes, foil-wrapped cheese wedges, and individual yoghurt containers that we could not afford during the year—our version of the Christmas orange.

Over the years, we created a Christmas Eve ritual of setting out a bag of toys that they had outgrown. They knew that Santa would take these with him and distribute them to other children. I figured that this would explain, if they asked, why the toys they received from Santa didn't come in sealed packages, weren't in pristine condition with all the decals ready to apply, and sometimes had missing pieces. They never asked.

Charlotte had now opened up the bright-pink box, and we filled up the plastic bin with water. She overlooked the package of fresh new decals and didn't seem to care about the orange accessories sealed up in plastic. She was focused on the flat plastic ring with holes in it lying on the bottom of the shallow tub. Tiny bubbles of air puffed into the two inches of water when she pumped (and pumped and pumped again) on a puffy plastic button. And that was it.

The disappointment on Charlotte's face was tempered by surprise. Of all toys to pick, this one certainly had a huge gap between the exciting hot-tub TV portrayal and its reality, a plastic bin with a manual pump that was less exciting than our rubber balloon pump. There was no Georgy Girl pop music playing in the background, no filter-enhanced visions of rippling water. The TV camera had spotlighted the smiles and long blonde curls of the young actress with her tiny hand delicately poised on—not frantically pumping—that button.

I could see Charlotte's mind working, processing, and within seconds, an adult-like sense of being duped passed across her face. She seemed to understand, and accept, exactly what had happened. She got what she asked for, but what she asked for wasn't what she got. This . . . this . . . was . . . *advertising*!

* * *

Over thirty years later, Christmas was approaching and I was chatting with Charlotte by phone. She was now almost forty and settled into her career. She was excited to tell me that for the first time in her life, her monthly income exceeded her expenses, a $600 surplus, thanks to her new job. For the past two decades, she had been adapting to a shoe-string budget, living well but with no frills beyond a safe apartment and quality hair-care products. I told her how proud I was that she had managed her life, her job, and her finances so well.

We talked about how many of her peers were facing an increasing debt load, and about how her priorities were different from theirs.

For the most part, Charlotte had led an alternative lifestyle, following her creative path of visual arts, writing, and social activism. It wasn't always easy for her watching her friends acquire homes and SUVs and vacations abroad while she stayed off the path of commercialism, partly for economic reasons and partly due to lifestyle choices.

She has never been easily influenced by consumerism and peer pressure. We laughed about the Barbie Bubbling Spa and how she learned, very early in life, that advertising can lead and mislead. She now seemed keen to find the toy online for the nostalgia. I wondered what her response would be seeing this well-marketed toy after so many years.

This prompted me to check out the TV commercial, now posted on YouTube. I was surprised to learn from its date that Charlotte's exposure to this commercial happened before she turned five. I reflected on Charlotte's precocious wisdom, her keen analytic mind, and her eventual graduate degree in rhetoric (the art of persuasion).

I laughed out loud when I realized the irony. Despite, or maybe because of, Charlotte's early awareness and distrust of TV commercials, the career path that now provided her comfortable salary was actually . . . marketing.

Her work was less brazen than the TV advertising that created false hopes in children. She got her start selling a retirement lifestyle to affluent seniors and moved on to promoting a small Canadian university. Unlike the Barbie Bubbling Spa, the amenities and services offered were as advertised.

18

Field Report

It had rained on and off all week. The kids were reacting negatively to indoor recesses and inclement weather lunch procedures. No one seemed dressed for the rain, and the school was very cold. The kids were cranky and were complaining of being sloshed by puddle-stompers. The teachers were exhausted and sick with colds, and their low energy level was resulting in a general gloom.

I was a student teacher in Mr. Lenton's Grade Two classroom at a downtown school. This was my first day in front of the class, although there was really no front of the classroom. I was on the carpet in one corner of the room, preparing to read a book I'd loved reading to my own children.

"But we already read that one," whined Robbie, looking across the room to the real teacher, Mr. Lenton. "Why isn't Mr. Lenton reading to us? I want Mr. Lenton."

Mr. Lenton, a tall, thin man wearing wool on this chilly September morning, moved a bit closer and tucked his reading glasses into the neck of his sweater. He remained silent. I was the teacher this morning, and he was letting me handle this challenge by this seven-year-old, who reminded me of Robert Godby in my own Grade Two class almost thirty years earlier.

"I'd like to read this book today," I affirmed in my most calming Mr. Lenton voice. "We have activities set up for you. I hope you can listen, even if you've read it before. You can join in if you want." I acknowledged, with a genuine smile, a little girl who was nodding vigorously. I suspected that she was one of the few whose parents read to her.

But Robbie wasn't buying it. He elbowed Chris, who was sitting beside him, and wiggled his ears, which always broke Chris up in laughter. It didn't take much to get Chris going. Now I had lost his attention, too. From the corner of my eye I could see kids squirming, so I started to read.

"Alexander and the Terrible—" Not half-way through the title, Robbie let a loud one rip. Chris fell over, lampooning death by flatulence, and, eager to regain control, I beckoned to him. He smirked as he joined me, leaving a bigger space for Robbie to fill. Robbie grinned and put his hands over his ears, rocking sideways toward the girls on each side and humming.

"Alexander and the Terrible, Horrible—"
Robbie was now drowning out even my teaching voice, which was stronger and slower. Without even glancing at Mr. Lenton, I looked right into Robbie's eyes and held them for what seemed like an eternity. I was struggling to tamp down my annoyance and hoped the look would get the message across while I breathed deeply, several times.

"Robbie, I can see that you don't want to listen to the story. Please go over to the reading centre and pick another book to read by yourself." He didn't move and didn't even glance at Mr. Lenton, who was now standing a bit closer to us, across the room from the reading centre.

Robbie crossed his arms firmly and sat stock still, his lips pressed together. I could see him shaking, just a little bit. Everyone was sitting still, for what seemed like minutes, waiting to see what would happen next.

I was stuck. Robbie was quiet, but he had ignored my request. The tiny girl beside him was visibly agitated. She got up and went quietly to the reading centre. I didn't know what to do, so I went back to reading. I had created a stand-off with Robbie, backed each of us into a corner, something Mr. Lenton would turn into a learning experience when we de-briefed at the end of the day. This would be a lesson for my field report.

As the book continued, more and more kids looked away from Robbie and joined me in the story. They chanted together the final lines of the book, "My mom says some days are like that. Even in Australia." Robbie was still not moving.

Hoping the kids wouldn't hear the tremble in my voice, I pulled out the 3-D thermometer activity that that would keep the kids engaged until lunch. I was excited about the activity, but still rattled by the incident with Robbie. I was not used to power struggles, and even I could see that this is what our confrontation had become.

The tension broke as the children headed to the activity centres, though I was not feeling victorious. The little girl who had left the circle was watching from the wings but did not participate. She had her arms folded, and her mouth was tight, a miniature version of Robbie. I kept an eye on her, and, as the kids put on their coats for lunch, she approached me, a frown on her face and her thin arms still crossed.

"I'm having a terrible, horrible, no good, very bad day." So she *was* listening to the story.

I took a plunge. I pretended to take something from my pocket, something so tiny it was invisible.

I tucked it into the child's hand, "Well, I'm having a good day . . . here . . . I'll share this with you and maybe things will change."

Robbie pointed his finger at me, "You didn't give her anything!" It was hard to keep a straight face, but this was serious.

I simply replied, "You don't think I did, but I'll bet she'll feel better by recess." And she did. She told me this later as she skipped off to afternoon recess.

* * *

That night I wrote up my field report for my advisors. What was being taught? the template asked. What was learned? I chose to write a self-congratulatory anecdote about being sensitive to the sad little girl, taking a risk at being playful. I had taught her that a bad day could be salvaged by a change in outlook.

What I wasn't ready to report was what Robbie and I had not learned that day. Robbie had felt anxious, Mr. Lenton kindly pointed out later. He was upset that Mr. Lenton wasn't the teacher anymore. He needed to feel secure, so he acted up, and when I tried to shut him down, he stood up to me. I failed to provide confidence, and I made the situation worse. I hadn't understood this. Standing up to a teacher was something I would never have dreamed doing. Only the bad kids acted up.

Now, as a student teacher, and despite my beliefs in encouraging children instead of controlling them, I had modelled Mrs. Nute, my own Grade Two teacher, not Mr. Lenton. Although I didn't yell or push Robbie, I tried to show him who was boss. I had turned it into a power issue.

My report ignored the learning situation with Robbie and highlighted my success with the little girl. I chose to report the positive aspects of the situation, not yet ready to face the difficulties I was experiencing.

Teaching in a community-school classroom was harder than it looked. There were thirty individuals to consider, and school was only one aspect of their challenging lives. I believed in child-centred learning, that each child learned differently and at their own pace. I believed that when kids "misbehaved" it was for a reason. I believed that they needed understanding, not punishment.

But I had made a mistake. Practice teaching involved mistakes, a lot of mistakes.

Mr. Lenton knew this. He stayed back, watching quietly, and let us learn for ourselves. He encouraged me to respect the young children as individuals and help them find their best selves. In the process I would find my own best self. It was learning by doing.

19

Prom Princess in a Convertible

My daughter Abby was going to the prom with Christian, a shy and serious friend from her class. She had picked out an inexpensive but suitably elegant dress in a gold silk look. She was a master of make-up, and her long auburn hair had been cut and styled. My baby was all grown up and finishing high school.

We were outside on the driveway when Christian arrived—in a convertible! It was a small British model, an MG perhaps. Definitely a two-seater. All consideration of its vintage, colour, and cool factor was overwhelmed by my terror. Christian's uncle was driving.

The uncle seemed like an ordinary, upbeat man in his fifties, and someone I wouldn't mind Abby hitching a ride with in ordinary times. The problem was, he hadn't considered the implications of Abby and Christian riding like a princess and her consort in what would, in a larger vehicle, be the back seat. The uncle had obviously polished the car and taken considerable time to set up a seat-like box covered in fabric. He seemed proud of his handiwork.

I looked at Abby, and she could guess my conflicting fears. The first, obvious to me, but apparently not to Christian or his uncle, was that there was no seat belt. At eighteen, she was liable for a fine for not wearing one, but that wasn't the problem. No, Abby was perched up high enough to ensure that she would be catapulted across the windscreen should a sudden stop be required at high speed.

The second fear, which I kept to myself, stemmed from social anxiety, and it prevented me from challenging the uncle, from pointing out his folly. He seemed alert to my concern, though, and offered Abby a scarf, as if it was her hair that was my preoccupation.

And off they went, Abby looking like Jackie Kennedy and me kicking myself for not saying something. My fear increased as they drove up the street out of sight, and I failed to convince myself that things would be fine.

We lived about ten kilometres from the school, and I could only hope that the uncle was taking quiet streets and not the four-lane Carling Avenue or, God forbid, the Queensway.

The next hour was one of the longest in my life, one of many waits for the telephone to ring with imagined bad news. Why did I not have the courage to stand up to some old guy I didn't even know?

But Abby was fine. A few weeks after the prom, she left home for university and from then on returned only for brief periods. Unlike me, she was a confident and adventurous traveller. She appeared to think nothing of exploring Europe, the west of Canada, California, Japan, and New Zealand. She even experienced Burning Man, the infamous counterculture event in the Black Rock Desert of Nevada.

Over the years, I got used to Abby's travel, but I have never escaped my racing imagination of doom. As far as I know, in her twenty years of adventure to date, Abby's closest brush with disaster was when her out-of-control bike with malfunctioning brakes raced downhill through red lights in San Francisco.

* * *

The night that Abby returned safely from the prom, I didn't ask her if they went on the Queensway. I didn't want to know. I think I will call her now and ask. She is currently in New Zealand preparing for a six-month stay on a blue-water catamaran in Fiji.

FLYING HIGH

FLYING HIGH

20

Anecdote and Antidote

Mr. Frank Rogers had snowy-white hair and exuded confidence that bordered on cockiness. He appeared throughout my life in various roles. He sang in the church choir, taught me to touch type in Grade Nine, and hosted our music exams at his home. But one fateful day, as master of ceremonies of a piano recital, he unintentionally embarrassed me with an anecdote but in the process provided me with a life-changing antidote to my terror of performing in front of others.

I was well into a decade of weekly lessons of the Royal Conservatory music program that my brother and I had promised to endure in return for my parents purchasing a Mason and Risch apartment piano. I took the promise and my music lessons seriously, despite a teacher who smelled like creamed corn and an older brother who would rather be out playing hockey than practicing. This meant that I had to learn three pieces for every one he learned so that we would remain in the same grade.

For this reason, we ran out of pieces in the Conservatory book, and my parents had to purchase additional, outdated books at a reduced price. Which is how I came to be playing at the recital from an out-of-date version that no one else had brought with them.

It was an easy piece, and I had practiced it to death. I had uncharacteristically thrown caution to the wind and left the book at home. I was used to full-body panic before and during these piano recitals, but the muscle memory from hours of practice had always paid off. Besides, the piece started off with a simple few notes in the right hand. What could go wrong?

I was wearing my favourite dress of all time, a deep-green, knit tube with short sleeves. It was the first dress my mother ever let me pick out. For some unknown reason she agreed to a style and colour that she would never choose. Its snug fit was not flattering and only provided encouragement for my brother to imitate me walking with my butt stuck out (I always leaned forward, always in a rush). But the colour was perfect.

The body-hugging dress was soft and comfortable after years of scratchy crinolines and itchy dresses my mother had sewed for me. I was completely unaware how its rich green complemented my freckled skin, strawberry-blonde hair, and blue-green eyes. I had not yet learned to appreciate these attributes.

Recitals were long and tedious, and parents felt compelled to politely sit through little kids stumbling over their pieces and bowing awkwardly. Leaving before the end was considered rude. The older students played at the end of the recital, a long and painful wait as my nervous system gradually eroded my confidence.

The longer we waited, the more nervous I got. I was expected to play my piece flawlessly, or at least with no mistakes obvious to the untutored audience. I always managed, until this time.

After what felt like forever, the recital neared its end. Mr. Rogers finally called me to the piano.

I went up and sat on the piano stool. I was glad that I had my weekly piano lessons on this Heintzman piano in the church gym. I didn't have to adapt to an unfamiliar room and piano. The golden face in a framed picture we called Jesus, Chairman of the Board, inspired confidence.

But I couldn't play a single note. I simply could not remember the note to start on. The one note.

The world stopped. A teacher who was blind and knew the score by heart kindly called out the note. The thing about playing by muscle memory is that the brain is bypassed. I still couldn't do it. I returned, head down, to my seat in the audience.

As the recital continued, the pieces got longer and longer. Would it never end? Finally, the last performer bowed, and Mr. Rogers graciously asked if I wanted to try again. I still couldn't face it. I declined with a shake of my head. I just wanted to get out of there.

But Frank Rogers, a Dale Carnegie man, felt compelled to tell everyone a story. He was enjoying the audience.

"When I was a young man, I saw a woman every day in the window of the piano store on the way to school," he started. I barely heard his introduction, deep in my misery.

"I wanted to learn piano so badly and decided this was the woman to teach me." Still not listening, I was hardly aware of the quiet around me.

"After two years, I got the courage to go in and ask about lessons. When she turned around, she was the most beautiful woman I'd ever seen. I decided right then that she would be my wife." I didn't care, I just wanted this to be over, I just wanted to go home.

"Her voice was as beautiful as she was, her diction perfect, and her manicured hands emphasized her charm. I was about to ask how she could play the piano with such long nails, when I realized that the music had continued even as her hands fluttered about.

"I never got to ask for piano lessons. The look on my face . . ." Oh, please, please, I prayed, make this story end.

The room filled with laughter at the punchline: "'Oh, no,'" she said, batting her brown eyes, 'I can't play the piano at all.'"

I was not laughing.

I'd like to believe that Mr. Rogers intended to reassure me—that it was OK to be incompetent if you were beautiful. But I didn't feel better. Green dress notwithstanding, I didn't feel competent, and I didn't feel beautiful.

I felt worse because being beautiful did not seem like a consolation prize. I wanted to perform for people with the ease and pleasure that he so clearly demonstrated. But I couldn't. Not yet.

* * *

Many years later, on a cold Ottawa evening, I walked into a conference room at Macies (now Best Western Plus Ottawa City Centre) at Westgate with a rolled-up newspaper in my right hand, whacking it into my open left palm.

"It is not fair, and I am furious!" I continued, whacking and chanting as I strode up the centre aisle to the front of room, past a group of twenty men and women dressed in business casual attire.

Continuing to whack, the eyes and ears of the audience glued to my face, I blurted out my anger about an incident that had occurred over twenty years before.

"I wanted the Cherry Blossom engagement ring!" Still whacking with the newspaper.

"It was a solitaire that was exactly what I had my heart set on!" Still whacking.

"In 1976, it was less than $200! We didn't have much money, but we could afford it!" Whack, whack.

"But my fiancé was determined to buy me a tiny one with hearts that he said he liked. But it's not him that had to wear it. And I know he just bought it because it was cheap. And he was cheap! He was always so cheap!"

My passionate expression of heretofore-unexpressed anger on the subject did not prevent me from noting the delight of people I had met only a few weeks before. They roared with laughter and profuse applause at my performance and, at the end of the evening, awarded me the best speech of the night.

This was the most exciting evening of the Dale Carnegie course. But there were twelve evenings in all, with varying themes and increasing periods in front of smiling and nodding faces. Each participant had to speak each week, and, if you missed a week, you had to come back to the next session and make it up.

We were encouraged to bring props and were delighted and moved by topics ranging from how to wear a sari to losing a son to addiction. One night I startled my audience with a talk about Wendo self-defence for women. I didn't just show the board I had broken with my hand, I demonstrated it. *Whack!*

That was not at all what I expected a Dale Carnegie course to be.

The fundamental principles of Carnegie's *How to Make Friends and Influence People* were simple: listen to people and treat them with respect. Unlike other public speaking courses that provide constructive criticism, Dale Carnegie courses focus on empathy and acceptance.

For twelve Tuesdays in a row, no one criticized. It was not about the content or delivery. It was about the courage to stand up in front of others and talk about something you were passionate about.

It was life changing. I learned to associate the adrenaline with pleasure, and maybe a tiny bit of power, freeing me to confidently tell my story to a crowd, large or small, friends or strangers. Now if I have trouble sleeping the night before a speech or presentation, it's because I am excited, not terrified!

* * *

When I was a child, the audience at our piano recitals and public-speaking contests were a mass of faceless parents expecting their children to outperform each other—it was a competition. The pressure was on me, an ordinary person, to be exceptional. To be perfect.

Dale Carnegie training, and other life experiences, taught me that, for ordinary folk, competence is a better goal than perfection. And I discovered that an enthusiastic and supportive audience is much more effective in developing competence and its running mate, confidence, than the pressure of a judging and competitive environment.

Perfection is an endowment that ordinary people cannot afford or sustain. Competence, by contrast, is doable, earned from allowing oneself to make mistakes in an environment of support and positivity.

I stopped playing piano at recitals not long after the fateful recital in my green dress. My last year at home, free from lessons, exams, and recitals, I enjoyed playing piano like I never had before. I continued to play for myself and my father and, after I left home, for close friends, children, and a local senior's day program.

Once I let go of perfection, I started to enjoy myself in front of an audience. I captured them with my enthusiasm, and they responded in kind. And that led to confidence.

* * *

The anecdote that Mr. Rogers told, all those years ago, failed to console me or reassure me, but his ease in front of an audience made a lasting impression. At the time I didn't know that he was a Dale Carnegie graduate, but eventually I made the connection between his confidence, his Dale Carnegie training, and my performance anxiety.

I had thought that the confidence Mr. Rogers demonstrated came from the perfection of his performance—his exemplary posture and diction—and that is what I had been seeking in the Carnegie philosophy.

Ironically, through my own training in the legendary program, I re-discovered what I continue to learn informally over my lifetime: letting go of expectations of a flawless performance is what truly frees me to enjoy myself and others. Just like Mr. Rogers did.

21

Ecstasy

As a child, I loved to lie on my bed daydreaming, listening to the sounds of summer. The occasional humming in the distance of small airplanes from our local airport was a special pleasure. It was a calming sound, but also something a bit otherworldly amid our mundane existence.

After I left home, my life started to broaden, and in my thirties, I got the chance to fly in a small plane. A World War II biplane offered short flights from the National Aviation Museum (now the Canada Aviation and Space Museum) just east of Ottawa. My three colleagues, Mark, Ken, and Jim agreed to celebrate our birthdays, which all fell around the solstice in June, with a biplane ride.

Mark had come up with the idea. Our newest clerk, he had attitude and a briefcase and talked constantly about airplanes. Ken, the project leader, was tall and lanky, with sparkling eyes and a laid-back chuckle. He loved new adventures. I was stretching my horizons after a decade at home with my children and another five finishing a degree by distance ed. I was game for some uncertainty that was slightly outside my comfort zone. Jim, a small wiry man with a full white beard and an artistic temperament, was up for any physical or mental challenge.

The biplane pilot met us behind the museum, and he was dressed for the part. I was particularly taken by his leather jacket and jodhpurs. He not only looked like a flying ace, he acted like one. His demeanour bespoke his confidence, and he could read a crowd.

We were to go up one at a time, in the passenger seat in front of the pilot. The ride would be customized for each of us. The pilot approached Mark first, sizing him up as the one for the most complex manoeuvres. He then met Ken's blue eyes with his own sparkle, promising a real joy ride. He reassured me gently, providing a thumbs-down signal as a visual safe word, and he left Jim for the final ride, allowing him to observe the rest of us before his own turn.

Mark jumped into the plane. In a matter of minutes, we could see that the pilot's competence matched his confidence and attire. This guy was the real deal and executed a number of turns, rolls, and a combination of the two. My heart started racing, and my stomach churned, even though I had been reassured that I would not get the full treatment. Mark returned to us, a giant grin on his face.

Ken was next, and his seemed to me like a more playful flight, with enough ups and downs to be thrilling. By this time, I was close to panic about whether I might be sick or faint in the air. All of a sudden, Ken had returned, his hair in disarray and a big loopy smile on his face, and it was my turn.

I hid my uncertainty behind a poker face and hopped up in front of the pilot. The adrenaline flooded my body, my heart pounded in terror, and my overloaded brain tried to warn me of dangers real and imagined. A bit late. The seat pressed my lower back as the plane ascended. My buddies grew smaller, and I naively tried to wave back at them. Damn! My arm nearly blew off, reminding me of my parents' dire warnings to keep our arms inside the car at high speeds.

By this time, we were heading up the Ottawa River, and I was starting to enjoy the ride. It was amazing to look down at expanses of river and trees and cityscape. I feared many things, but I loved heights. It was remarkably loud and startlingly beautiful. The plane seemed to hover, the sparkling blue of the river and the green of trees and lawns below, the Parliament buildings in the distance.

Then, it was quiet. Oh, crap, oh, crap, crap, crap. What was happening? The pilot was sitting behind me. I had no visual clue, no indication of how serious the problem might be. The plane was moving forward. It was not falling. There was no emergency! It's like we were drifting on the air. It felt light and gentle and ethereal. This, I realized, was gliding!

Just as I gave in to the unexpected feeling of peace, the engine roared again, and we headed back, but the pilot had not finished with me yet. I hadn't reached my thumbs down threshold, and it was time for something completely different. Now, the pilot tipped the nose down. As I was gaining confidence, he combined it with a slight turn.

It wasn't much of a manoeuvre, but it was enough to throw me for a loop. I escaped, for an instant, my perception of up and down, totally outside the normal experience of gravity. This was clearly the climax of the trip. Before my body could cry out in panic, it was over, and I was left with something beyond relaxation, beyond peace. It was ecstasy.

Back on the ground, I didn't even notice Jim's turn. I was too busy telling everyone about how incredible the ride was—orgasmic is the word I used. My experience had loosened my tongue as well as my body, and my colleagues laughed with me. Then, before we knew it, we were stuffed back into Jim's little black car, heading back to another afternoon at the office.

It's been almost twenty-five years since that awesome day, and few experiences in my life have topped the intensity of that flight. I faced the fear, I delighted in the sheer expanse of sky, open air, and landscape below. It was the unexpected but liberating jumble of all three for an amazing moment in time that I remember as ecstatic.

I still love hearing small planes in the distance on a sunny day. And now when I hear a small plane overhead, I always look up, and sometimes, to my delight, it's a biplane.

22

How to Lie with Statistics

Have you read the little book *How to Lie with Statistics* written in 1954 by Darrell Huff? Presenting data is a tricky business, especially health data, which can be complex and misleading. The message isn't always what it seems. Changing the scale on a graph, for example, can make a modest trend look huge. There are many technical details—bias, stratification, and causality among them—to consider. The reader is easily deceived by false results.

In scientific literature this deception is usually accidental, which is why peer review is critical. Sometimes, though, "creative" use of data presentation is purposely meant to mislead. Alternative facts aren't a new phenomenon.

As a clerk-turned-editor in several health-analysis groups, I was encouraged to participate in analytical discussions of our work. Questions, no matter how naive, were welcomed. I learned through experience how to interpret statistics and hone my critical-thinking skills.

In the early 1990s, before e-mail and the Internet took over our lives, these review sessions helped analysts share knowledge and stimulate discussion. Moreover, the presentations were a social outlet, especially for the biostatisticians, who spent a lot of time quietly at their desks. And there was the food.

Most of the time, the snack was something sweet: doughnuts, muffins, or the occasional home-baked treat brought in by a student or female employee. The men contributed, too, but usually something store-bought.

The most memorable of these events was the time a young grad student I'll call Doug brought in fruit tarts. I have no recollection of what Doug's topic was or whether his charts made sense. The discussion was no doubt lively. As usual, the peer review was serious and the atmosphere collegial. But something seemed different. There was a festive atmosphere that didn't match the gloomy February weather. Perhaps it was the novelty of the shiny fruit tarts.

Doug had set out the tarts in the back of the stuffy room where we would see them on our way in. The fluted tart shells were filled with creamy custard and topped with a glistening layer of colourful fruit: mandarin oranges, raspberries, and blueberries. I had seen this luxurious type of dessert at the gelato store on Preston Street but had never bought one. They were new and impressive and not yet available in grocery stores.

As I stumbled past a flipchart to get a seat for the presentation, I could see the tarts in my mind's eye, but at my seat, it was too far to see what the flipchart was all about. No matter how interesting Doug's work was, all I could think about were the tarts.

* * *

As the presentation neared an end, I couldn't help mentally counting the people around the table, hoping there were enough tarts for the latecomers. Ken, who had arrived during the questions and answers, was standing in back with the tarts at close range.

The discussion over, the crowd stalled as we filed past the flipchart on our way to the back of the room. My heart was racing in anticipation as I perused the dozen Polaroid photos of Doug, his tall, slim body in an apron leaning over the counter or stove, in the various stages of preparation.

I examined the making of these gorgeous-looking specimens while worrying that there would be none left. Here was Doug, in a red apron, rolling out dough on the countertop. In another photo, he was pulling a tray of tart shells, perfect in shape and not at all burned, out of the oven.

In yet another, Doug was stirring the custard in a double boiler on the stove and smiling to the camera. He was still smiling as he carefully laid out blueberries and raspberries on the custard, now set to perfection. I wondered how long the custard had taken to cool. And then there was the glaze. This was just unbelievable.

When did he have time to do this? Most of my colleagues were madly putting together their slides well into the night before their presentation. And here was Doug, not only making these creations, but documenting the process. And why?

As I came to the last photo of Doug placing the tarts lovingly into a Tupperware container called a cake taker, I looked over to see if the crowd had subsided and if there were still tarts left. They warranted a bakery box with a gold seal on it, I thought.

But wait a minute. Was it possible that they had come from a bakery box? I heard Ken's hearty laugh as he gestured towards the flipchart with his long middle finger, glistening where he had licked off the fruity glaze. His eyes sparkled more than ever as he patted Doug on the shoulder with the same hand and started to guffaw. I clued in on the joke. Doug hadn't made the tarts at all!

It dawned on me that the photos were all staged. It was a trick that Ken, our playful team leader, would appreciate.

* * *

When I got back to my office, the taste of custard and raspberries still in my mouth, I thought about how Doug had carefully crafted the story, with evidence, of how he had made these lovely tarts. He had even transferred them from the bakery box into a Tupperware container.

I settled back into the manuscript I was reviewing, smiling about Doug's trick but now aware of its underlying message: healthy skepticism is an asset for scientists and health editors. Doug had provided fake evidence, and at first I had bought it. I had ignored a basic question I learned early in my days as an editor: Does it make sense? Did it make sense that Doug had made the tarts, despite the Polaroids and his confidence-inducing smile?

In the boardroom that day, I would not have hesitated to question Doug's presentation of his scientific findings, but I didn't challenge his capricious photo documentation of those eye-catching delicacies. I just chuckled and chowed down.

23

Love at a Price

My love affair with Steinway pianos was ignited on a snowy day in January. My daughter Abby and I were wandering past the piano store on Wellington Street, the one with the stylized harp and golden text "Steinway & Sons" on its door.

We were aware that she was heading home the next day, and we hadn't had time for piano shopping. Abby was living in New Zealand, building a music-teaching career. She wouldn't be back to Canada for another three years. She had been pestering me for several years to upgrade our piano. My beloved piano, Abby claimed, was not worthy of my competence.

I was resisting. I had discovered my piano thirty-five years ago in a large warehouse of refurbished instruments and purchased it for $600, no tax. This was all we could afford in 1978 with me pregnant and my husband unemployed. Our rented house was small, but there was finally room for a piano of my own. The one I chose was not particularly attractive, with square edges and dull brown finish. Its name had been stripped from its cabinet. But it had a full, generous sound and the loose and friendly "touch" of my grandfather's Heintzman piano.

As our family grew and we moved to larger houses, the piano was more than a piece of furniture. Even Charlotte, often driven to distraction by her sister Abby's practicing, loved to sing while I played.

As I approached my retirement years living alone, Abby said I owed it to myself to buy something better. I had been loyal to my old piano, despite its cracked wood frame, the result of the dryness of our first little house. For years, my piano technician would sigh and replace tuning pins for the lower notes, aware that it would not hold its tune for long. I got used to its honky-tonk sound.

Now, Abby said, I could afford better.

* * *

Into the piano store we went, past the pricey grands placed by the front window where they were visible to passersby. We headed towards the lone upright, a shiny black one, tucked against the side wall of the showroom. A woman called Sheila greeted us gently and started to detail the quality of the Steinway piano, focusing on its back first.

Pointing to the solid-looking wood with pride, she explained how the construction of the frame would withstand the years, which caught my attention right off, considering the sad condition of my own in that regard. After showing us the hexablock tuning pins, she allowed the information to sink in while she played the expensive instrument. Then she led us over to the window and picked up a model of the piano's action. She demonstrated how the keys were weighted and delicately balanced on a round fulcrum, giving the Steinway its characteristic responsiveness when striking the keys.

By the time Sheila was describing the unique resonance of the Sitka spruce wood brought in from the north to make the tapered soundboard, my brain was full, and the details were getting jumbled. Wisely, she handed us a video to take home. It showed the hand crafting of Steinway pianos in New York. It also showcased major performers, like Lang Lang, who were loyal to the Steinway brand. She provided a glossy owner's magazine with ads targeted to a wealthy readership. Finally, Sheila walked us around to the Steinway's poor cousins: the Boston, made in Japan, and the Essex, assembled in China. I wondered whether these models had the qualities she had just shown us.

We had now been in the store well over an hour, and it was dark as we headed out into the storm. As we strolled across the park for our final supper together, the wind whirled and so did my thoughts. I couldn't believe Sheila had spent so much time talking to us. Was she having a slow day, or did we look like we could afford such an extravagance?

I had been aware of Steinways, Glenn Gould's piano of choice for performing, since I was a teenager. My father, who surprised me by listening to classical music in later years, once told me that he had watched Gould's Steinway being manoeuvred over the seats into the high school auditorium for a concert.

But $20,000? That was almost as much as I paid for my car.

* * *

Over the next weeks, I test drove the pianos I could afford. I played Yahamas alone in a quiet back room of the dealer and Kawai pianos, the ones with plastic parts, amid the hubbub of Saturday students in a crowded storefront. I even tried a Hardman at my piano tuner's showroom while he went upstairs to make tea.

The Yamahas had an amazing touch and were brilliant in sound, until I hit a bass note. A piano technician later told me that they are great for a few years and then deteriorate badly. The Kawai pianos played deliciously and felt like butter under my fingers, but when I went back on a quiet day, the sound was disappointing. I was hesitant about their plastic parts, despite the benefit of resisting humidity changes. Charismatic salespeople and alluring prices of February notwithstanding, there was no perfect piano in my price range.

Then one day late in February, I happened to pass by the piano store on Wellington Street again on a lunch-hour walk. We public servants were heading into a year of layoffs, and I had decided to take a break from the tension of waiting for the cuts to materialize. As I passed the piano store, I decided to treat myself to a few delicious minutes at a Steinway keyboard.

A rich, walnut-stained Steinway was now against the side wall, the ebony piano shoved aside against a partition. The moment I heard the sound of this new arrival, I was transported. I had never played a piano with such resonance! I didn't even want to try the black one again.

After a few minutes, the same gentle Sheila appeared and offered me some information about this delightful instrument. It was a trade-in, three years old. This was good news. Maybe I could afford a Steinway after all. The soundboard on this particular model, the K52, was unique in an upright, being close to the size of the sound-board in a grand piano. This explained its amazing resonance. The cabinet was from the Jewel Collection, a glossy walnut finish with a narrow inlay giving added richness to its visual appeal.

As I forced myself back to work, reality set in. Sheila had cautiously but respectfully revealed the asking price of this dreamy instrument, $25,000—even more than I expected to pay for the brand-new ebony Steinway. Well that is that, I thought. Who in my income range would pay over $20,000 for a piano, and a used one at that? More than twice the cost of a new Yamaha.

And so began twenty-four hours of despair tempered by manic infatuation. Despite the price tag, I knew this was a rare opportunity to purchase an exemplary piano. I tried to justify the expenditure with rational arguments: I lived modestly, took transit instead of owning a car, rarely indulged in retail therapy or costly vacations. Would I regret this extravagance when I might be laid off by year-end? Or could I get a bargain because it was a year of financial uncertainty in a city of public servants?

The truth was that I really really loved this piano.

The next day, a bundle of nerves camouflaged by my tough negotiator skin, I headed up to the store after work. It was worth a try. The markup on Steinways was likely considerable, and they had more give financially than I did. I played for yet another half hour to build up my courage. It was getting dark, and I was feeling mellow as my best friend entered the store to provide a second opinion. As I played, my friend walked towards me, stopped, and let out a soft slow laugh of pleasure. This was it. I called Sheila over.

Sheila listened carefully without a word, then went to the back room to discuss my offer with the owner. I had made it clear that I absolutely loved this fine instrument, but I couldn't pay more than $20,000—taxes included. As I sat alone at Sheila's desk, glancing over at the piano's delicate inlay, I braced myself for a no or a counter offer I would not be able to consider. On one hand, it would be a grave disappointment. On the other, it might rescue me from the folly of my uncontrollable desire.

After a long and painful few minutes, the owner himself came out and sat down at Sheila's desk. He had heard me playing, he said. I knew by this time that this instrument, new, would cost over US$30,000. He now told me with a dead-serious face how these pianos, unlike cars, hold their value. This was a very special instrument. I held back the tears of disappointment, a dream denied. He smiled and said, "It's a deal."

* * *

A week later, the piano movers tipped my old piano onto its side, its bottom now cracked from end to end. I watched from my picture window as they moved it to my garage and wondered if it could even be tuned again. Maybe I should have taken up the offer to put it in the dumpster behind the piano store.

But then my new piano was in my living room, and I felt shy and overwhelmed. Change is hard for me, even a good change. When the movers left, I crept out to the garage to see my old piano, thinking that despite its astounding resonance and snooty reputation, the Steinway really didn't have the voice and touch of my old derelict. I shivered in the cold and played a few chords. Despite the wonderful new piano, I was still attached to the voice of my old friend of three decades, the response of the now ice-cold keys under my fingers.

It took a while for me to get used to my new piano. My old one would be long gone before I accepted that the old comfortable relationship had been replaced with a shiny newer one. Despite its scratches, the three-year-old Steinway was, by comparison, fresh and new, inside as well as outside. The hammer felts were clean and white. Bright red felt strips set off the shiny golden strings. And there was no smell of dust.

Almost identical in colour and shape to my old no-name piano, the Steinway looked far more beautiful. The shiny finish reflected the light, the delicate grain enhanced by a narrow strip of inlay that framed my music scores. And, of course, the sound reverberation literally made me shiver with delight, especially when it caught my friend's happy laugh from across the room.

* * *

Meanwhile, I had offered up my old piano to anyone willing to risk its age and cracked frame. Although several people expressed interest, it was Tiffany, a woman at my work, who came to take it home.

It was bittersweet watching my old piano hefted out of my garage and up into a truck. A tiny woman with pink hair, Tiffany watched as three friends tipped the huge piano up on its back for the drive to its new home in the country. She told me she had opted to cook steaks for her friends because piano movers cost too much.

A few days later, she sent me a photograph of the piano and her cat. The piano had survived the trip. I hoped she could afford to have it tuned, that she would accept its honky-tonk sound.

I had never even asked if she could play the piano. But I hoped that no matter what, she would love it for many years, just as I had.

Meeting David Johnston

I almost blew my chance at a most memorable day in my working life. The word had come down from senior management that our project group had been selected for an award. It was 2013, and we public servants were beyond disgruntled with the Prime Minister. I didn't want to shake the man's hand.

Luckily, it dawned on me that the Prime Minister would not be making the presentation. It would be the Governor General, His Excellency the Right Honorable David Johnston. Now there is a man whose hand I looked forward to shaking, although in my mind he was still just David Johnston.

I had been following him in my university's glossy alumni magazine as he became the president of the university and then Governor General. He was described as a man of the people, a dignified but folksy individual who cared about the marginalized. Not quite Jack Layton, but still.

My cynicism about the government of the day was shared widely at work. In the previous few years, the powers-that-be had adamantly rolled back the evidence-based decision-making and data analysis that we had worked so hard to develop during my whole career.

As a former Health Canada employee, now at Statistics Canada, I was beyond offended and actually frightened about the fall from grace of data. We believed that population-based data provided the key to improving the health of Canadians. And yet here we were.

Worse, the rumours that would rudely awaken all public servants from complacency had come true. More than half of us, having worked our way to being indeterminate—permanent employees with pension and benefits—were now slated to fight for our jobs. We had a week and little text boxes with a two-hundred-fifty-word maximum to prove that we deserved our job more than the other equally offended individuals we worked beside every day.

So, no, I didn't want to shake the Prime Minister's hand or even be in close proximity to him. Even thinking about him put my stomach in knots.

David Johnston, on the other hand? It was worth putting on a suit for him. A simple black pantsuit would do, dressed up with a bright apricot blouse. As it turns out, my blouse matched the country-fair striped wallpaper in the large reception room where we would spend most of the morning.

We arrived in taxis, taking in the majesty of the trees and stone walls of Rideau Hall as the red-uniformed staff opened the doors of our cars. Inside, we joined the mass of public servants in an immense foyer with portraits of historical figures looking down on us.

After checking out the cloak room and bathrooms, we ascended an ornate set of stairs and filed into a large, solemn space with removable chairs. Our team of ten sat among a few hundred men and women, both teams and individuals. For about an hour, the project descriptions in English and French demonstrated to us that it was an honour to be there. Public servants are a lot more productive and creative than many Canadians think.

The next part of the event—waiting in the cheery reception hall with the tent wallpaper that matched my blouse—seemed even longer than the presentation ceremony. I would rather be at work than chatting idly with people in a noisy crowd, I thought, refreshments notwithstanding. I was annoyed at what seemed like an unnecessary warning sign not to set glasses on Glenn Gould's piano.

The crowd thinned ever so slowly as teams were called into an adjacent small room. I had no idea what was happening or how long it would take. I was getting anxious. On my own, I would have bailed at this point, but I was taking it for the team.

Suddenly, the staff hustled my team into the adjacent room, which was filled with camera gear. They parked us on chairs around His Excellency. Why such a rush after the long wait? The staff and photographer bustled us into place for the group photo.

It was here that I could have used a bit of time to linger. On the walls were several huge canvases by William Kurelek, two behind us and several others within our vision beyond the cameras. I knew there would be tiny children and adults hiding in the colourful prairie fields like a *Where's Waldo?* book.

Feeling like a deer in the headlights of these treasures and the flash of the camera, I realized that the photo had been taken and now we would have a chance to shake David Johnston's hand. He had a personal question for each of us. I wish I could remember what we talked about. His authentic smile and warm demeanour assured me that he was listening to my answer.

The rituals over, I headed across the room to view the paintings more closely. And I was abruptly accosted by the public servants responsible for moving us on and out the door. Just doing a job, in this case traffic control.

Before I knew it, we were ushered downstairs back to the foyer, handed a plastic award in a paper shopping bag, and sent back to work in a taxi.

* * *

Despite my cynicism about the government of the day, I enjoyed the opportunity to speak to the Governor General in person. I hadn't mulishly stayed back at the office with the dozens of people who did the work but were not invited to the ceremony. It was an honour to receive the award and an unexpected pleasure to linger beside Glenn Gould's piano and almost contemplate several works by my favourite Canadian artist.

Despite the government's apparent cynicism about our contribution, we had succeeded in liberating Statistics Canada data, a long-awaited milestone in providing free access to information about Canadians. Not long afterwards, the Prime Minister was replaced, a new Governor General moved into Rideau Hall, and I retired from the public service.

People come and go. Priorities change. Sometimes just staying the course and taking a risk in face of cynicism pays off.

Canadians got free access to statistical data, and I got my day at Rideau Hall.

MOVING ON

MOVING ON

25

Making Drapes

It was time to say good-bye to the drapes that had graced my windows for over twenty-five years. I had come to love these bright, flowered fabrics as much as the view of trees they framed, and I would miss both.

I had made the drapes myself when we first bought a house with two picture windows. Our previous homes in older neighbourhoods had provided lots of smaller windows to practice on. Purchasing bargain fabrics by the yard, I had experimented with colours and styles. Being an at-home mom imposed the need to economize but provided ample time for shopping, planning, and sewing.

With a new house, we were still penny-pinching. The Bouclair store on Merivale Road held me captive as I perused bolts of fabrics folded around cardboard panels. The clanging sound of their metal stands was a calming background music that drew knowing looks from other fabric addicts.

I compared colours, textures, width of the fabrics, and of course, the price per yard on a small ticket tucked inside the bolt. Inevitably I made my purchases from the huge table with discounted fabrics on giant rolls.

My projects became more bold and adventurous, including neon-orange shower curtains and a French blind of purple polar fleece, constructed from small pieces of wood, cup hooks, and white plastic rings.

And, inspired by our large new windows, I ventured to the wall of shiny cotton drapery fabric. Up on the wall, floor-length samples hung in soft pleats. One particular pattern, though garishly pink with huge roses, was toned down by a teal sash, bringing out the matching accent flowers. Could I adapt to pink, a colour that still makes me slightly queasy?

Standing across the store from the display, scouting around the discount fabrics, I looked back at the wall and asked myself whether I would regret a change from my dated preference for oranges and purples.

Drapes require a rectangle of fabric three times the width of the window to create generous pleats. Eighteen yards, at five dollars a yard, was a small fortune. I watched with apprehension as the clerk flopped the bolt over and over, unleashing the massive length of fabric and making the final cut.

The fabric for the second set of drapes was an easier purchase. Wine-red was my favourite colour, and, although the luscious fabric I spotted at $2.50 a yard on the discount table also had large, pink roses, I succumbed.

* * *

I had made numerous pleated curtains in the past. It was sort of a game for me. I loved the planning part. Each pleat required several inches of fabric folded into ridges. Sewn in place where the hook goes, a generous pleat gives a nice drapey look, so I had learned not to skimp on fabric. Calculating the distance between the pleats tickled the part of my brain that loved small mathematical challenges.

For years, my friends had pestered me to use pleater tape. There was no fussing and sewing of pleats, they said. I could sew on a strip of pleater tape and stick the hooks in. No one told me that I would need to repeat this every time I washed the drapes, which adds up over twenty-five years! Did other people even launder their drapes?

Moreover, the hooks were prone to popping out just as you were nearing the end, as you were trying to hang the curtains on a ladder with your arms holding the weight of the drapes above your head.

* * *

It was a sad day when I was preparing my house for sale. I had discarded drawers of fabric left over from my sewing projects and given away boxes of trim and other notions. As I sorted through scribblers with plans, I came across the sketch of my drapes in my sewing drawer under my shears.

Now the real-estate stager was recommending neutral tones for the picture windows. The wine-red drapes had been in the living room for the past decade to coordinate with a wine-coloured couch and chair from my grandmother's parlour that had been reupholstered at considerable cost to celebrate a promotion at work. The drapes with the big, pink flowers now framed the maple tree at the back of the house.

Both were still in good shape. Although the shiny sizing was long gone, the colour was still close to the original, thanks to liners that protected them from the sun. My staging consultant had advised neutral curtains, however, and, with more money than time, I purchased my first ready-mades from the local mall.

The blandness of the new drapes was blinding, and they hung awkwardly, an inch shorter than my custom drapes. Would anyone notice? Like my blue, sponge-painted bathroom and red bedroom upstairs, the gaudy drapes had to go.

As I tucked my two sets of pink-flowered drapes and the dreaded pleater hooks into a green garbage bag for the St. Vincent de Paul store, I hoped that someone who liked bright colours would discover them and extend their life for another few years. They had stood the test of time and outlived several carpets and couches. They had seen my daughters growing up and my friends consoling me over my divorce and my father's death.

They had cheered me up for another fifteen years living on my own, and I would miss them. My new apartment was equipped with vertical blinds, modern but lacking that indefinable quality that coloured fabrics possess. I gave my drapes a final farewell hug and ran quickly upstairs for a cup of tea and a few tears.

26

The Mystery Building: A New Perspective

It was a rainy afternoon, and the bus shelter was crowded. Feeling tired, I decided to stand a bus-length away, under the Queensway overpass where there was a bench out of the rain. As I absentmindedly put my keys into my bag and dug out my bus pass, I glanced back along Preston Street towards Carling to check for the bus. A completely new building right at the end of the street took me by surprise.

The building rose out of the trees at the end of Preston, near Dow's Lake. From where I stood, I could see the top ten stories but not its base. It was large and square and grey, with an aerial on the roof, and it was completely finished, unlike many buildings under construction in the area.

For the past five months, I had been spending many hours exploring the Preston Street area, not to mention time waiting at bus stops. I was enjoying the newness of retirement and living in this vibrant and changing community. Like me, Little Italy was in transition. The community, an aging Italian main street, was evolving with remarkable speed to a rapid-transit hub with upscale restaurants and high rises popping up everywhere. I was evolving too, moving back downtown to an apartment, after twenty-five years spent raising a family in a 1950s suburb further west.

From the comfort of my new couch and recliner, I had been following with great interest the construction of new towers going up in my new neighbourhood. I had taken time to peruse websites that chatted about the progress of these buildings. I had even watched the demolition of the Sir John Carling Building, an "implosion" that had spread dust over several blocks, although this was before I moved to the area.

I was confident that I knew the landscape. The grey building could not have been there the previous day. And yet there it was, perfectly visible despite the rainy weather.

I made a final scan of the buildings in the area. I shook my head and came back to reality. Buildings don't appear from nowhere.

The bus arrived, and I huddled on. As I sat down, it hit me. Was this the Dunton Tower at Carleton University? It was!

In my mind, the Dunton Tower, which I still thought of as the Arts Tower, wasn't grey and square. It had a reddish cast when viewed from my window at sunset. In my mind, it was not in line with Preston Street, but when I consulted a map, it was.

Standing under the Queensway on a grey day, the concrete walls highlighting the building like the mat on a painting, it did look grey to me. Nestled among the street and trees, it did look shorter and wider than viewed from the red Muskoka chairs across the expanse of Dow's Lake.

It was all very puzzling and awe-inspiring. Objects are modified by perspective and the surrounding context, like a diamond on a velvet cloth or two lines that seem different in length when one has arrow tips and the other arrow tails.

* * *

Over the next weeks, my thoughts turned to how a change in context was affecting my internal perception of myself and my life. Many things I was certain about were turning out to be untrue. Sometimes it was a simple fact I had believed or a word I have been using wrong for decades. Other times it was learning something startling about a person whom I'd known most of my life. Sometimes that person was me.

I had fretted for years about moving from the quiet security of my single home of twenty-five years into the noisiness of an apartment building. I got stuck, fearing the stress and the hugeness of it all. Then I moved. I found a quiet building. I survived, adapted, let go of the past. And found adventure in a new neighbourhood.

I established new routines: laundry without steep stairs to a cold basement and garbage disposal in my slippers without regard to weather or day of the week. Freed from the home-maintenance treadmill, I started to visit Preston Hardware just for fun.

Of course, unpleasant surprises arose. My dark, overstuffed furniture, lovely on the blonde hardwood of my 1950s home, looked out of place against the modern bamboo flooring and trendy grey walls. The best spot for the couch had the worst view.

With change came a shift in perspective. Things looked different in new surroundings.

In my house, I took comfort from the familiar: the same line of trees behind the same brick houses, the same bus to the same office, the same food from the same cafeteria. It felt safe.

From my apartment I could see more sky, filled with cranes and high-rises. Unexpectedly, I began to delight in change: the daily weather, the seasons, even the high-rises-in-progress above the tiny houses. I took in Italian street festivals, religious processions, and Ferrari parades, and enjoyed the profusion of ethnic and theme restaurants.

Things were different from what I expected. I was seeing different things. I was seeing differently.

27

Trouble with a Water Flosser

I spent months, yes, months, trying to master the art of using a water flosser. My dental hygienist had been pestering me to use one for my gum health, and I finally gave in.

I learn quickly in general, but it takes me a long time to get used to new gadgets. I take time to read instructions and in this case even checked out an online video.

I was skeptical. The video showed a man I'll call Brian in a suit. Like his attire and pristine bathroom, his flossing experience looked too perfect to be true.

The water did not flow down onto his clothing or anywhere else in his bathroom. This was not my experience.

* * *

It took me several months to get started. The first step was ignoring the box in my bedroom. I was busy moving, so I had a good reason to put it off.

Settled in my new apartment, my guilt got the best of me, and, as my next step, I got the pieces out of the box and discarded all the plastic. I read the manual and cleared a place for the machine on my expansive bathroom counter.

I came back to it a few days later. The manual advised the high-pressure setting to prepare the tool for use. I aimed the flosser in the direction of the drain. I won't pretend my drain was pristine, because it wasn't. The flosser blasted the gunk off the little plastic thingy that holds up the stopper. Unfortunately, the little moldy bits didn't go down the drain. They landed on the surface of the sink.

The gunk didn't hit the flosser tip, but I worried it might have while I was trying to find the water pressure slider or the pause button. As a neurotic with an overactive imagination, I can attest that it amounts to the same thing. One way or the other, I couldn't un-see this grossness. It stuck in my mind even as I set the flosser aside for another few weeks before attempting the next steps.

* * *

Getting the implement into my mouth and keeping my mouth slightly open sounded easy but required a few more attempts. And that doesn't count figuring out how to aim the tool at my gums.

Brian's flosser was on the counter to the right of his sink. Luckily, he was right-handed. I am also right-handed, but there was no room, or electrical outlet, on the right side of my sink.

I got off to a bad start because the annoying coil of tubing that joined the water unit on my left to the wand on my right was directly in the line of fire—I mean water, which was dribbling from my slightly open mouth.

I quickly learned that I would need to move everything that was within three feet of the sink or dry it off afterwards. One way or the other, the mirror and my glasses would both need to be cleaned.

As I tried to focus on aiming the water into my mouth and not across the bathroom at large, the awkwardness of hitting my gumline distracted me even further. Hitting the sweet spot between the gum and teeth on my left side with the tiny stream of water was an immediate success, but the dexterity required for the right eluded me. How could it be so different from using an electric toothbrush?

Well, for one thing, my electric toothbrush didn't shoot water all over the place if I missed. And my toothbrush didn't hit that ticklish spot on the roof of my mouth. The flosser did. My response to that was to open my mouth without thinking. This had a predictable result. I was glad I was not wearing a suit like Brian.

* * *

The next challenge was swallowing, or rather avoiding the reflex to do so. I knew it wasn't a real problem, like the warning not to swallow toothpaste. But in my focus on keeping the tip aimed at my gumline and not my ticklish spot, I accidentally closed my mouth for too long.

The water kept coming, and then—I swallowed! And I couldn't un-swallow! Somehow this triggered my fear of swallowing those little bits the dentist polishes off my fillings. I doubt that Brian was thinking about his dentist, but I wondered about his swallow reflex.

And the noise! I still hadn't got used to that.

When I had first turned on the water flosser, I was so startled by the rattling noise, *rattatattatatt*, that I let go of the button on the wand. That stopped the water temporarily but the not the sound, which got even louder when paused. *RATTATATTATATT*, like a miniature jackhammer.

* * *

I really did try. Every few weeks, I'd soldier on. But it was a vicious circle. I'd turn on the flosser, and the noise would trigger my startle reflex. I'd frantically let go of the button, the noise would get louder, and the water was shooting out again, hitting the ticklish spot. My wrist would unflex, and the plastic tubing would recoil like an out-of-control fire hose. The tip was no longer pointing in the expected direction. And my mouth was open.

I should have quit at this point. Outwitted and outmanoeuvred by this deceptively benign gadget, I felt unbelievably incompetent. Oh, to be Brian, calm and dry, mastering such a simple procedure. In the face of defeat, the only answer was distraction. I found myself thinking about the goop in the sink instead of the pesky water flosser. The image from weeks ago was as clear as the obsessive thought about whether I should have cleaned the drain.

I tried to calm myself by narrating this new and difficult process in my head. Before I knew it, I was composing this article in my head instead of paying attention. It's not hard to guess what happened when I lost my focus.

This article survives, but the water flosser did not. I confessed to my hygienist that I had failed. Another year passed, and a new dental hygienist started at me again. This time the COVID-19 pandemic struck just as I was testing out a new model. A valiant start, but I didn't need much of an excuse to abandon the new flosser on my counter for another four months and counting.

28

Hidden Treasure

On Doors Open weekend in Ottawa, thousands of people line up to see inside buildings they pass daily without a second thought. This year, I was determined to visit at least one, too.

The Canada Council Art Bank, open for one day only, has no line outside. Arriving at the corner of McArthur Road and St. Laurent Boulevard, a wide and noisy thoroughfare lined with huge car dealerships, I wonder if I have the wrong address. But then I see a large banner announcing the Doors Open event.

Tucked between two parking lots, the Art Bank is inside a nondescript, one-storey building with a weary picnic table in front. The welcome is low-key. Staff with name tags hanging from their necks are quietly talking to visitors, but there is no guided tour, no map, no indication of what I am about to see.

I join a few visitors along a narrow corridor past a series of alcoves that remind me of library stacks. Interspersed with a few pieces of artwork are colourful panels promoting the Art Bank: "the collection belongs to all Canadians"; "individuals can benefit from art rental"; "it costs as little as $3 a day."

Next is a large, open space with couches and people examining several large canvasses, one of which is a painted Google search about Indigenous peoples, and about fifty smaller framed pieces. I focus on a collection inspired by sushi. It turns out to be a playful view of

Canadian cuisine: blueberries, Tim Hortons doughnuts, and what appear to be wieners wrapped in rice and thin layers of cabbage.

Hidden in one corner of this gallery space is the entrance to an immense warehouse of sculptures and 3-D art in a variety of media. One of the first is a clear Plexiglass wagon sitting on a lower shelf, but soon the sheer volume of objects overpowers my attention and clouds my memory. Dozens of pieces sit randomly on the painted concrete floor, and more are hidden in boxes on shelving units, each about thirty feet long—there must be thousands of cartons hiding unique Canadian treasures inside. The labels and pictures on the boxes hint at the variety of a collection too extensive to grasp. A big-box store for art.

By now, I am completely overwhelmed. My brain is tired, and my heart is full. It takes time to examine, to absorb, to wonder. I want to come back another day, but there isn't another day. I head sadly toward the door, hoping that the Art Bank will be on the list next year.

Then, on my way out, I discover that I have missed the best part of the event because I have not strayed off into the alcoves that looked like library stacks. These house some of the 17,000 pieces of art promoted by the colourful panels, but it has not occurred to me that it is open to the public.

The alcoves house white-mesh sliders, about fifteen feet long and ten feet high, with heavy metal frames and large handles facing into a centre aisle. They sound and feel like oversize patio doors when they are pulled out to expose four to six pieces of art with small tickets and QR bar codes. The panels completely block the aisle when fully extended, so visitors pull them part-way out, from both sides of the aisle, creating a maze-like passage to the far end.

I retreat to the edge of the room and watch. The crowd, suddenly increasing in size, is as diverse as the artwork. A little girl in a striped dress has her neck bent back fully to look up at the brightly coloured houses several feet above her mother's pointing finger. A tall, mature woman is clutching a catalogue, and a young couple is using a cell phone to scan the QR codes.

It requires all my strength to slide the heavy panels out, then back in again. Soon I am physically tired and choose to just look at the works that others are pulling out. I wander through five or more alcoves—I soon lose track—with at least one hundred sliders in each, unsure whether I am going around in circles. I can't even begin to appreciate the wealth that surrounds me.

Despite the deep sound of rollers, the scene is hushed, like a cathedral. Most people are looking and gesturing but not talking. A few consult quietly with staff who are standing by laptops searching the Art Bank database. The room has the intimacy of a gallery despite its warehouse size. Gauges on the wall indicate controlled temperature and humidity. It is a comfortable space.

It feels a bit unreal to stroll amidst so many pieces of Canadian art. It's almost beyond belief that ordinary Canadians have access to this secret stash.

As I leave the building, I thank the curators, who seem astonished by the turnout. They have run out of catalogues and still have several hours to go. I learn that they have hosted smaller events, but for decades this amazing repository of Canadian art has mostly been hidden from sight, exposed only to its small staff of curators and managers.

Every day, thousands of people in cars and buses pass this humble little building. It is not the National Gallery, with its glass towers and gleaming hardwood floors and natural light, and it's not on the radar of residents or tourists. But on this single day in June, more than a thousand ordinary Canadians wandered into the rich treasure housed by the Canada Council Art Bank and owned by us all.

29

My Filter Queen

A mysterious ad in the Help Wanted section of the *Brockville Recorder and Times* intrigued me. I was looking for a quick way to make money in the evenings during my last year of high school now that I had finally stopped taking piano lessons and had more time to make money for university.

I don't think they said it was selling vacuum cleaners over the phone, but that's what it turned out to be. My job was to sit at a desk in a lightless room with an old rotary telephone and a small column of numbers cut from the telephone directory. I would call each number in turn, using the name from the list.

We would offer a set of steak knives to entice the homeowner into a no-risk visit by our sales team. It wasn't actually a team, just a bunch of young guys who made a lot of money if they got a sale. Better yet, I made a lot of money if they got a sale.

I was rewarded with $2 if the person accepted a home visit and $5 if there was a sale. To put this in context, my other part-time job in a pharmacy paid almost $2 an hour, and the going rate for a job with a college diploma about $5 an hour.

So, if I was lucky—and I was—I could make what seemed like a princely sum in a short period of time. My paychecks often exceeded those of my part-time job in the pharmacy, and the one exciting aspect of the job was seeing that my calls had resulted in a sale.

I didn't stay in this job long. Though it was lucrative, it was painfully monotonous. I didn't talk to the other callers. I just did my job and went home. More important, I sometimes recognized the names because Brockville was only just big enough to be a city. On the rare occasion that I called someone I knew, I desperately hoped they wouldn't recognize my voice. Luckily the script didn't call for me to introduce myself by name. I didn't know much, and cared even less, about the product I was flogging.

* * *

A few years later, I was a married student on a limited budget, and we needed a vacuum cleaner for our first apartment. By coincidence my brother-in-law was now selling Filter Queens. He had exemplary sales skills, even if he pushed his credibility with an anecdote about selling a machine to a family with a dirt floor. My husband and I, though resistant to his brother's charm, were still intrigued by the product. We soon found ourselves owning a refurbished vacuum cleaner. Yes, it was a Filter Queen.

I had experience with a fair number of vacuum cleaners because another way to earn a lot of money quickly was housecleaning. None of them had come close to my grandmother's ancient GE canister machine that my brother used when we were at the farm in the summers. The Filter Queen's suction was even stronger than this gold standard and looked more durable with its shiny chrome bin and rubber-and-bristle brushes.

The machine was expensive, but it was worth it. I never doubted that my first vacuum cleaner, purchased in 1976, would last a lifetime.

Over time, we bought filters and paid for an occasional cleaning, and my husband patched up the end of the faded hose with duct tape. Once, I pulled too hard on the cord and had to replace the plug. But the machine was, for the most part, problem free for the next forty-five years.

My Filter Queen came with me to my new apartment. After the dust cleared from my move, I suddenly realized how old my vacuum cleaner was. Influenced by the newness of my building, I started to fuss about the vacuum's aging wiring, wondering whether this machine would really last a lifetime.

It turns out that I was more fragile than the machine. A few shoulder injuries and an aging back started to cry out for a lighter model. I looked around and found a trendy vacuum cleaner with the same cyclone-type technology and no bags to replace.

I was happy with my new vacuum cleaner. As promised, the machine and wands were much lighter, the tools were more flexible, and it even had a retractable cord. Its cheery red design fit into my bright new home.

Still, it took a while to shake loose my attachment to my old Filter Queen. I don't use it anymore, and my back is grateful. But I do miss its solidity and shiny chrome wand. I wonder if anyone wants a forty-five-year-old Filter Queen. For now, it's still taking up space in my closet while my bright, new vacuum sits in the corner of the bedroom.

HEADY VERSES

HEADY VERSES

It's Hard Being Neurotic

Off to the pool with my flippers,
Bathing gear, scarf, and ice grippers.
The stove off, checked twice.
Heat, windows, checked thrice.
Door locked! Look down—at my slippers!

Bronson Johnson-Swanson

Swan E. Swanson has wed John E. Johnson.
She's now Swan E. Johnson [dash] Swanson.
They'll soon have a son,
Whose name will be fun.
He'll be Bronson John Johnson [dash] Swanson!

Have You Seen the Muffin Man?

I saw an old guy at the pool
Wearing bike shorts so tight (although cool).
And above he wore nuffin'
So he looked like a muffin.
No, really, he looked like a fool.

Dust on the Cake

Emerging at length from shadows of past,
We dine this evening together at last.

I drink in, unembarrassed, this wonderful creature.
Savouring with delight his every feature,

Listening with rapture, the music, his voice,
I feel, now at last, we have made the right choice.

I rise in a dream from fine food and good drink,
Imagining, naively, he shares what I think.

Looking back, I see clearly, my impression was just
On the cake, a fork stenciled in sugary dust.

I saw first his sugar, then speared by his fork,
I heard him say loudly, cheque in hand,
   "Well, that was over-priced, wasn't it?"

Seen in the Playpark of My Imagination

Mediocre being superlative and Superlative being mediocre
trying hard to hardly try
observed
on
a
teeter-totter

Attention!

Very far back from the uncertain danger of the unforgiving edges,
you stand in safety, until, drawn by the unseen,
unwitting, move towards the unknown.
Attention! Caution overtakes.
Back out of sight, still,
natural force
of erosion
edges,
down
you
go
.

.

.

Fossils in the Wind

Like dinosaurs on a rampage, transition
Stirs up things,
Things breaks down,
Forward pushes things,
Around things moves,
Things behind leaves,
Like footprints in the quicksand, changes

Kathy White is a retired public servant living in Ottawa. She completed degrees in English and Education off-site by the age of thirty-five, but her two daughters and her work colleagues were her main teachers. She continues to take interest courses at local universities with a growing circle of people who love writing. She enjoys riding the O-train and sitting in the red Muskoka chairs beside Dow's Lake.

The cover art was graciously provided by my daughter, Charlotte Clarke. She and her sister Abby spent countless hours reviewing and editing this manuscript. Love from your mummy and friend. Your expertise and kindness made this book a success.

Tim Niedermann polished this manuscript. Thanks, Tim, for smoothing my prose, tidying my descriptions, and enhancing my phrasing.

Heartfelt thanks to my life writing instructors and support groups. My deep appreciation to my second home, the Ottawa Public Library, for supporting "In the Company of Writers," where these stories took shape.

Glenn Sweazey has been a dedicated leader with limitless literary lessons and prolific praise. I am so grateful for the safe space to learn the craft. I am much obliged to Connie, Dave, Irene, James, Janice, Joan, Joanne, Marie-Andrée, Pat, Pearl, Philly, Stephen, Yasodhara, and the many others who shared early versions of these stories.

Martha Musgrove, you showed us how to create an anecdote and critique gently. Thank you for introducing me to my first loyal readers, Jessica, Holly, Mark, and Mary. We shared lively discussions, wine, and cookies!

Thank you, Anna Rumin, for your stimulating writing prompts and dedication that led to this unexpected collection of works.

ACKNOWLEDGEMENTS

Giant distance hugs to my reviewers Elizabeth, Joanne, and Nancy, and to the many other friends who kept me going.

Special hugs to my loyal friend with the soft slow laugh of pleasure, for flowers and space while I was completing this collection.

And finally, my sincere thanks to all who see themselves in these memories and reflections, especially Helen, Robert, Richard, Thomas, and Pam. Peace to those who are with us in spirit: my father Raymond, my grandparents Alfie and Edith, and also my erstwhile underappreciated teachers Mildred Hyde and Frank Rogers.